A PASS
FOR LEARNING

CELEBRATING 80 YEARS
OF NIACE SUPPORT
FOR ADULT LEARNING

PRESENTED BY
Howard Gilbert and Helen Prew

NIACE
THE NATIONAL ORGANISATION
FOR ADULT LEARNING

First published in Great Britain
2001 by
The National Institute of
Adult Continuing Education (England and Wales)
Leicester

Copyright © 2001 NIACE

ISBN 1 86201 128 1

Designed by Geoff Green
Typeset in Minion
Printed in Great Britain by
Alden Press, Oxford
Production for NIACE: Virman Man

A PASSION FOR LEARNING

CONTENTS

Acknowledgements   vii

Foreword   ix

Preface   xi

Introduction: view and overview – a subject for celebration   1

THE ORIGINS OF NIACE
Lord Haldane; the Haldane Trust; the British Institute of
    Adult Education; Sir William Emrys Williams   15
Fusion not fission – the BIAE Secretary remembers   27
Reminiscences concerning NIACE and its predecessors   29
The beginning of the National Institute of
    Adult Education   32
An Inspector recalls those early years   37

CHEFS IN A HOT KITCHEN
Recollection of Edward Hutchinson – mentor and
    family friend   41
Edward Hutchinson – Secretary, 1949–1971   43
Arthur K Stock – Director, 1971–1988   50
Alan Tuckett – Director, 1988–   56

GATHERING STORMS –
HOPES AND REALITIES, 1970–1990

NIACE during the 1970s and 1980s   63
How they brought the good news from Queen Anne Street
    to Leicester   68
A friendly lodger (ACACE) from 1977–1983   71
Wise Presidential guidance in a time of turbulence –
    1988–1994   80
Sir Winston Churchill on adult education   85
REPLAN and UDACE: The 'Baronies'   87
A broadcaster's perspective   98

ROLLING BACK THE DARK CLOUDS

Adults and Higher Education: the NIACE role?   105
International aspects and exciting developments: 1975–1995   110
Growing independence in Wales:
    NIACE Dysgu Cymru   115
Drama, growth and fun – NIACE in the 1990s   122
A right to read   131
Tailpiece   141

References   142
Abbreviations   146

Many other reminiscenecs have been sent by various other contributors to this volume. NIACE is delighted to make these available on the internet, at the following web site: www.niace.org.uk/publications/anniversary/

ACKNOWLEDGEMENTS

T HE FOLLOWING PERSONS have generously provided articles, offered comments and information, or reviewed draft texts and made suggestions. To all, NIACE and the Editors give their very grateful thanks for excellent support, and acknowledge a considerable indebtedness to them.

Grace Atkin;	Sir Roy Harding	Charles Nicholson
Maureen Banbury	Saskia Heasman	Douglas Payne
Guy Baxter	Richard Hoggart	Joan Raymond
Alan Chadwick	Arthur Humphreys	Naomi Sargant
Peter Clyne	Patricia Hurst	Richard Smethurst
Margaret Davey	Dewi Jones	Ann Stamper
Konrad Elsdon	Henry Arthur Jones	Arthur Stock
John Farago	J Rendel Jones	Judith Summers
Howard Fisher	Derek Legge	Alan Tuckett
Paul Fordham	Brian Leighton	Tony Uden
Bernard Godding	Harold Marks	Hazel Ward
Don Grattan	Stephen McNair	Graham Wilkinson
Brian Groombridge	Geoffrey Mills	David Wiseman

The Editors also acknowledge help from:

The Arts Council Archive at the Victoria and Albert Museum; The Tate Gallery; Bristol University Library; The National Library of Wales, Aberystwyth; the NIACE Archive; Hertfordshire County Council Library Services.

FOREWORD

Richard Smethurst
President of NIACE 1994-2001

I T I S M Y P R I V I L E G E to be serving as President of NIACE as it marks its 80th birthday by publishing this fascinating collection of reminiscences and essays. My first duty is to thank everyone who has contributed, but especially Howard Gilbert, who conceived of the project and has driven it through to completion with patience, good humour and steely determination.

As Howard says in his overview, this is not a careful analytical and critical history of the role of NIACE and its predecessors in shaping policy and practice in adult education – though anyone writing such a study will find much of interest in these pages. Nor is it a *festschrift*, contributed by pupils and colleagues to mark the retirement of a distinguished scholar. For far from beginning to wind down in wisdom and maturity, NIACE is experiencing the most rapid growth in its history, and coping with the immense constitutional, managerial and cultural changes which are involved, many from the margins, as it were, to the heart of government planning and policy-making. Yet, as in the best *festschrift*, there are some contributions here which will become required reading. Mostly, however, these are speeches at a birthday party for an old and trusted friend, the odd sharp phrase or risky anecdote carried along in the joyous celebration.

Passing through a similar – though lesser – 'decade birthday' recently I found that instead of an autumnal regret, two other, linked, emotions dominated. First came embarrassment, then astonishment: I didn't feel so old: indeed it was only yesterday that I was much, much younger, and I still felt like that inside, whatever my present physical state. NIACE, by contrast, can rejoice in its 80th birthday, for it remains as vigorous it its outward actions as it is in its internal discussions. 'Older and Bolder' might be the motto of the whole organisation, not just one of its important projects. I demit office, as I commend this book with affection and pride.

PREFACE

Howard Gilbert

T HE WORK IS DONE; it is to be published in book form, and on the web-site – I suspect the first National Institute of Adult Continuing Education (NIACE) publication to be so presented. For me it has been an enjoyable, interesting, absorbing and sometimes fascinating experience; those are the right adjectives to which ought to be added a sense of exhilaration that it is now finished. The preparation time has been one during which old friends were contacted and many old acquaintances renewed. It has proved an opportunity to connect with the new generation of professional people who are responsible for the education service to adults today, and to learn a little of their tasks.

I am grateful – and in considerable debt – to those who have provided articles and photographs for text or illustration. Equally I have appreciated offered advice, information and assistance sought from colleagues from time to time; these have added to my knowledge and appreciation of the subjects and the editorial task. In many instances this has enabled the inclusion of significant elements, or added important matters of substance that might well have been overlooked. Not all commentaries or suggestions have been included; nevertheless, I am very appreciative of every observation made because each has enlarged some part of my own understanding of events or situations to which they relate.

A particularly special word of gratitude must go to Helen Prew, who began this task as the Director's Professional Assistant and is now Policy and Communications Officer at NIACE. She joined the early planning stages, has fulfilled the role of progress chaser, has been an invaluable liaison contact for me, ensuring – as need arose – that critical information, help, and 'that right person' at NIACE was alerted to assist the process forward. Without her careful help scripts, in various states of readiness, would not directly have ended up on the 'system'. With her enthusiasm and efficient management of the NIACE end of the business the stages towards publication have been smooth and comfortable.

I must acknowledge the generous help provided by Helen Biggs, NIACE Librarian and Archivist. She has given me much assistance during visits to NIACE in search of answers to questions that were, on occasion, obscure or uncertain in their focus. Equally I am grateful to Brian Leighton who, due to family pressures, withdrew from the main task, but with the diligent assistance of Patricia Hurst, Librarian at the John Rylands Library, Manchester, secured access to some early British Institute records. My thanks to all three for their support.

The 80th Birthday of NIACE – 28 May 2001 – almost coincided with Adult Learners' Week (ALW) which ended on 18 May and was just eight weeks later than the incorporation of the new, national, Learning and Skills Council (LSC). This is an 'executive non-departmental public body' which took over the training functions of the Training and Enterprise Councils (TECs) and the funding responsibilities of the Further Education Funding Council (FEFC). It also has responsibility for adult community learning and youth, being advised in this connection, by two statutory committees. The former Secretary of State, David Blunkett, has described the Council's creation as 'revolutionary'; for the first time in the history of English post-compulsory further education, there is a national body for the organisation, planning and funding of adult learning opportunities. This 80th Anniversary publication appears at the end of an era of kaleidoscopic development; that conclusion is also the start of a new epoch in the education of adults. In offering the customary greeting to NIACE, 'many happy returns', it is appropriate to look ahead to a prospect of another rich, diverse birthday publication in 80 years' time, on 28 May 2081!

Leverstock Green, Herts
September 2001

VIEW AND OVERVIEW

A SUBJECT FOR CELEBRATION

Howard Gilbert

Quince: *'Here is the scroll of every man's name, which is thought fit
through all Athens, to play in our interlude before the duke and duchess
on his wedding day at night.'*
(A Midsummer Night's Dream, Act 1 Scene 2)

T HIS BOOK (and the NIACE web pages) is a collation of reminiscences, recollections, anecdotes, thoughtful and witty essays, and
personally remembered events or incidents during the life of
NIACE from 1921 up to its 80th Anniversary on 28 May 2001. These come
from members who experienced the occasion or who saw or heard it
happen. They are drawn from members' own resources, and from the
NIACE archive in Leicester. Turn the pages to find some high octave
moments, some low or muted passages, a few quavers and crochets and
numerous mellifluous sweet, harmonious scores that provide point and
counterpoint to the 80-year span. This is not a history of NIACE; that has
yet to be written. But this celebrates its rise at the time of hope and
enthusiasm following the Ministry of Reconstruction's 1919 Report, under
great patronage, to the year 2001 when the entire schema for the education of adults is taking a new, distinctive and potentially exhilarating
course.

The order of presentation is broadly chronological in both media.
However, a liberty with the timescale has been taken here and there,
where coherence demanded variation. There is more written text about
the earlier days than of recent date; that is inevitable. Nevertheless the

balance is more than re-dressed by Judith Summer's fine article *Drama, Growth and Fun – NIACE in the 1990s* which focuses the great changes during that decade, conveying the sense of the time when she was an Executive Member (from 1982) and its Chair from 1992 to 1999. To this view, Stephen McNair – Head of Research until 1999, and now Professor of Education Studies at Surrey, adds two dimensions: *UDACE* and *Alan Tuckett.*

NIACE – the youthful years (1921–1949)

On 28 May 1921 at 29 Tavistock Square in London 60 to 70 professional persons met together to form the British Institute of Adult Education (BIAE). Most of them were from the University and Responsible Body tradition of liberal adult education of a non-vocational character. The Chairman was Dr. Albert Mansbridge; the patron, Viscount Haldane of Cloan who became the Institute's first President, and thereafter Life President, until his death in 1929. Haldane was a powerful, political figure; a Cabinet Minister in Liberal and Labour governments; a lawyer with much experience of arguing the case for extending university education and securing charters for provincial universities. More detail of his involvement is given in the article, *The origins of NIACE.*

Members decided that BIAE would not become a Responsible Body with class organising authority, but that they would seek to secure the 'university connection' standard that Haldane had insisted should be a prime criterion of course level. The Institute would concentrate its energies upon influencing structures, services and individuals who taught. A number of key members – Mansbridge among them – were also holding appointments upon the Board of Education's own Adult Education Committee. This body, representative also of public authority and university adult education, advised the President of the Board upon the development of appropriate services for the education of adults. Its terms of reference were remarkably similar to those given by Shirley Williams, Secretary of State in 1977, to the Advisory Council for Adult and Continuing Education (ACACE). The Committee was expected to encourage growth and development, with proposals for the most effective use of resources, in all forms of adult education including that by the LEAs. However, because of its composition, it progressively concentrated its concerns upon the needs and interests of the 'university connection' and the Responsible Bodies. This practice inevitably influenced the fledgling British Institute.

The bias changed over time, partly through the activities of W.E. Williams who became BIAE Secretary in 1934, and witnessed the signing of the Haldane Appeal Trust Deed. He persuaded the Institute's Council to support a proposal for an exhibition series called *Art for the People*.

Harold Marks, NIACE Individual Member, and former Staff Inspector for Adult Education, in his contribution *An Inspector recalls those early years*, speaks of Williams as a rather 'flamboyant figure', and notes some of his achievements. Williams himself became Secretary-General of the Arts Council in 1951, and has described *Art for the People* in *Adult Education* (Volume 50, No. 4, 1971) which celebrated 50 years of the Institute's work.

During the Second World War, the Institute (BIAE) had maintained the level of its work in line with the 'university connection' and the standards of the Responsible Bodies. However, much of its funding had come from the Pilgrim Trust, achieved through the advocacy of Williams, and strongly supported by Dr. Thomas Jones who chaired the Trust. He was a member also of the Committee for the Encouragement of Music and the Arts, (CEMA), set up by the Institute at the invitation of the war-time President of the Board of Education, and through which many of the funds for the art related activities were channelled. The Board also made cash grants. Nevertheless, the money resources of the Institute were somewhat diminished when hostilities ended, as David Wiseman, former Secretary in succession to Williams in 1946, infers in *Fusion not fission – the BIAE Secretary remembers*; his personal contribution to this celebration.

As one response to the 1944 Education Act, local authorities had encouraged the setting-up of the National Foundation for Adult Education (NFAE). This came into being in 1946, with Edward Hutchinson as its Secretary. The organisation paid £10 per annum subscription to BIAE as an Associate Member, and the two organisations, with several members in common, began discussions, which were to lead to their merger in 1949, at Buxton.

NIACE – Nuptial, not nativity, and what followed

Derek Legge, today an Honorary Life Member of NIACE, represented the Tutors' Association when the jointure occurred in 1949. His *Reminiscence* of the occasion and those who came, is an important personal record. He recalls also an earlier conference when adult educators assembled in 1943 to discuss the White Paper which eventually became the basis of the 1944 Act. Henry Arthur Jones, in 1949 recently appointed as Staff Tutor at the Manchester Extra-Mural Department, also went to Buxton. He writes about it in *The beginning of the National Institute of Adult Education* and points out that everyone present assumed the event was a marriage, not a birth. The 'slightly stooping man' that he saw mixing with the delegates was Edward Hutchinson, the Secretary-Designate of the new organisation.

Brian Groombridge in his *Profile of Edward Hutchinson* says that, at the time of the merger, 'there was no certainty that this good idea would succeed'. Henry Arthur Jones thought also, that an 'accountant and economist' was an unlikely combination for success in the leadership of the new Institute. He adds, however, in the event, it was an 'inspired choice'. Saskia Heasman (née Mills) knows about this time; she was a child at school, and her parents lived with Edward Hutchinson. Mr and Mrs Mills confirmed the record noted by Brian Groombridge, that there was much discussion in the household as to whether the sacrifice of a secure job as Deputy Treasurer for Surrey, would be worthwhile for Edward in the long run. Saskia contributes a short *Memoire* about the man who became, in 1949, the first chief officer of the NIAE.

The 1960s, 1970s and early 1980s

Don Grattan, British Broadcasting Corporation's (BBC) Controller of Education Broadcasting during the 1960s and 1970s, worked with Edward Hutchinson to assist broadcasters to develop educational (adult) television and radio programmes. He had a long association with Arthur Stock too. His *Broadcaster's Perspective on NIACE* incorporates several recollections of critical moments in the development of the Literacy Programme (Adult Literacy Resource Agency) and the BBC's contribution to that, with the TV series *On the Move* which introduced the then unknown Bob Hoskins as the lead man. Grattan was appointed to ACACE in 1977, and became the first Chair of the Unit for the Development of Adult Continuing Education (UDACE) in 1984. Stock speaks for himself, in a wide-ranging article that covers the period of his Directorship, which began with the high hopes of a major advance for adult education when the Russell Report was published. This proved a false dawn, although the appointment of ACACE (Advisory Council for Adult and Continuing Education), (1977–1983) raised hopes again that were to be dashed once more.

Paul Fordham, then Professor of Adult Education at Southampton, was Chair of the Executive in the 1970s, and Chair of REPLAN (an education programme for assistance to unemployed people), knew Arthur Stock well, and has provided a *Profile* of the man, and his concern both nationally, and on the international stage, for those who would most benefit from adult education but who were frequently deprived of the opportunity to secure it. The early hopes of Stock's time were finally dashed when ACACE was ended by Sir Keith Joseph in 1983. However, due in some measure to the energies of the Director and his Chairman, REPLAN was established, whilst the recommendations of ACACE were translated marginally, and the Basic Skills Agency (BSA) was created out of the Adult Literacy and Basic Skills Unit (ALBSU). At about the same time, UDACE was formed. *REPLAN* and its achievements are described by Tony Uden, Director of the programme for its seven-year term; *UDACE* and its success are discussed by Stephen McNair, Head of the Unit until it merged with the Further Education Unit (FEU) in 1992. (McNair and Uden were retained by NIACE respectively as Head of Research and Associate Director.)

The article *A friendly lodger* outlines the work of ACACE between 1977 and 1983. The Council's administration, under John Taylor and Martin Warburton, had 'friendly lodgings' at the NIACE Leicester headquarters. The arrangements enabled effective information sharing and liaison between the two bodies – the former a national, voluntary charitable organisation and the latter a Government-appointed body. Arthur Stock became an Assessor to the Council, contributing to the close association between the two that these arrangements made possible.

Wise Presidential guidance in a time of turbulence

Sir Roy Harding, who succeeded Lady Bridget Plowden as President in 1988, shortly after the new Director, Alan Tuckett, was appointed, remembers his first years as ones of change and transition, which followed the Agency era of Arthur Stock.

His *Personal letter* – a response to the invitation to recall his time with NIACE – is reproduced in full, apart from a brief preliminary paragraph. The letter illustrates the struggle by NIACE to maintain itself, and the search for new directions allied to a changing status to that of a company limited by guarantee. This shift of emphasis became essential. The problems were compounded, initially, with the restructuring of further education following the 1992 Act and the progressive loss of the 'Agencies' during the period of the Presidency.

Discussions that I have had during the preparation of this celebration tell of the thoughtful care and wise guidance that Sir Roy brought to the Presidency, and which helped to pave the way for the great advances that came in the second half of the decade. NIACE will long remember this President and his work for them.

Change during the 1990s

International contexts and interests were part of the Institute's tradition from its first manifestation in the British Institute, and the influence of Albert Mansbridge. Edward Hutchinson and Arthur Stock continued that interest; Alan Tuckett has enlarged this through, among much else, the development of a world-wide dimension to Adult Learners' Week. Howard Fisher, Associate Director from 1975 to 1995, charts much of that interest in *International aspects and exciting developments*.

Within the United Kingdom devolution has brought more than polit-ical change. In the mid-1980s, NIACE established a Welsh Committee and subsequently NIACE Cymru was formed with an office in Cardiff. Dewi Jones, addressing the annual study conference, forecast *Growing inde-pendence in Wales* and the emergence of *NIACE Dysgu Cymru* (NIACE Learning Wales).

The 1990s also have seen the expansion of connections with the higher education sector. Haldane's vision, in the 1920s, was to secure, for the education of adults, the 'university standard' in their learning. Stephen McNair, in a short essay *Links with Higher Education,* outlines the achievements of the Institute in creating a stronger association with the university sector.

Judith Summers was Chair of NIACE Executive throughout much of the time of transition and advance. In *Drama, growth and fun: NIACE in the 1990s* she attributes part of NIACE's achievement to the development of skill in handling the 'role of political criticism'. It is worthwhile here to notice evidence of that skill and its subsequent effect upon parliamentary discussion and debate. On Thursday 20 April 2000, in Committee the fol-lowing was printed in *Hansard,* attributed to Tim Boswell, former Con-servative Minister of State at the Department for Education and Employment (DfEE), and now on the opposition benches. He said:

> *There were some exchanges in the other place on this matter and initially the Government got off on the wrong foot. NIACE's com-ments on the quality of the Government's response to probing amendments in Committee were uncharacteristically censorious. I am not making a qualitative judgement but if NIACE is upset, that usually suggests that there is a problem or insensitivity. It is not impossible to give assurances that are reasonably satisfactory and it is important that they should be given.*

The challenge facing NIACE now is to ensure that the new LSC and its satellites truly secure a comprehensive approach to adult learning wher-ever it takes place.

Finally, a *Profile of Alan Tuckett,* NIACE's present Director, who was appointed in 1988, and whose task – as Sir Roy Harding says – rapidly became a difficult one with the loss of what George Low and the journal

Education called the 'baronies': ALBSU, REPLAN and UDACE. As Judith Summers has indicated, this gave space – in the longer run – for NIACE to 're-invent' itself. The author of the *Profile* is Stephen McNair.

He ends on a note that represents a concept of adult education that has been constant since the days of Albert Mansbridge, and before his time too. Derek Legge refers to it in his *Reminiscence*: he says that the meeting at Buxton (1949) was the occasion when he made contacts who became, subsequently, lasting friends. Mansbridge saw the British Institute as a branch of his larger World Association for Adult Education (WAAE); as one consequence friendships would be formed and international harmony enhanced.

Basil Yeaxlee, the editor of the *Handbook and Directory* from 1928–29, had a similar view about lifelong learning, underpinned in his case by a sense of its potential spiritual quality. The concept is apparent in the Women's Institute movement as readers of Anne Stamper's book, *Rooms off the Corridor* (1998) will be aware; it infused – and continues to do so – the activities of organisations as diverse as the Workers' Educational Association (WEA), and the Educational Centres Association (ECA). Each of NIACE's chief officers, in their different ways, have endorsed this and expressed it in their family life as being fundamental to a fulfilling life course. The immediately contemporary view of lifelong learning tends to focus upon its utilitarian value, NIACE may yet find a further challenge to accept within the context of the LSC: that lifelong learning is also an important medium for the sustaining and enrichment of cultural and social living.

The Web-site…serendipity

> *"…thou shalt like an airy spirit go – Peasblossom! Cobweb! Moth!*
> *And Mustard Seed!…Ready, and I, and I, where shalt we go?"*
> (*A Midsummer Night's Dream, Act III, Scene I*)

Among the many pieces sent by members of the Institute, responding to the invitation, are a number that are delightful, self-contained re-collections, narratives and even legends. These will appear on the web-site – which during the year 2000 attracted 25,000 enquirers – to provide a rich gathering of experience, service offered, momentary remembrance, and enjoyable occasions or events that make up the adult education kaleido- scope that is NIACE and its story. First, however, a birthday greeting from someone who is a friend of many years to NIACE, Maureen Banbury HMI.

> *To NIACE on its 80th birthday.... Greetings. It goes without saying, of course, that my links with NIACE go back a long way and that HM Inspectorate have always valued their advocacy for the adult learner, in what-ever context.*

Brian Leighton, Individual Member, volunteered with me, to be one of the production team, launching the project with an article that was printed in *Adults Learning* (March 2000). In it he described how and when NIACE encouraged him as a relative 'new boy' to work with adults. Part of his writing is included in this section: *Professional perspective: A varied career in the education of adults.* In similar vein another profes- sional found his life course touched by NIACE; Douglas Payne, reflects upon *I wonder if....*

The role and influence of NIACE Presidents has often been signifi- cant and on occasion, critical for the organisation. Each has brought dis- tinction to the position. In this appreciation, Henry Arthur Jones recalls the different qualities of *Presidents* he knew.

Lady Plowden, a kind, thoughtful, intelligent President, sadly, died several months ago, as this publication was in preparation. Peter Clyne's *Obituary* note, published first in *Adults Learning*, (Vol 12. No.2), is included here in tribute to a woman who did so much during her life for education's many aspects, especially adult learning.

Anne Stamper represented the Women's Institute (WI) on NIACE Council, joining for the first occasion when the addition of 'C' (for 'Con- tinuing') was being debated and wondering what, exactly and precisely, it was all about! She mentions the help she received from Lady Plowden which enabled her to become rather more than *Being a humble Member of Council.*

J Rendel Jones, Honorary Treasurer of NIACE in the late 1960s and early 1970s, appreciates the contribution to education made by Bridget Plowden, and recalls also some of the more difficult moments for NIACE:

People, money and the Common Market, reminding members of the international dimension to the Institute's work. Hazel Ward, previously Dean of Adult Studies at West Herts College, remembers Howard Fisher's (Associate Director) help in a brief letter to the editor which tells how he created a link for her in India. An example of *NIACE providing professional support.*

Conferences, especially those in earlier years, are recalled by Margaret Davey, Principal of the Cit Lit.

Bernard Godding remembers one in which an elected member caused quite a ripple in the hall. He tells the story – a vignette – under the title of *Chocoholic*. Bernard, who today is Chair of the Educational Centres Association (ECA) – a national charity that promotes partnerships between students and tutors, in educational settings, tells of a slightly odd coincidence involving *Edward Hutchinson: in time and space.* The special educational needs of adults received close attention during Arthur Stock's Directorship. Bernard Godding completes his tally of recollections with a note about *Making a difference,* a project within NIACE that opened a new door to these special needs.

Ministerial visits to the NIACE annual conferences were welcomed and appreciated; on occasion they were also frustrating to the participants and their presentations bland in quality. Henry Arthur Jones' commentary, *Ministeria,* illustrates some of the colourful moments of the 1960s, 1970s and 1980s.

NIACE exists to promote the cause of adult learners, among other responsibilities. Two learners have contributed to the record: Charles Nicholson, retired adult educator and now in the learning seat, discusses his experience; John Farago, a retired Chief Executive, asks whether we should have a *Royal Society for Learning.*

The 1950s and 1960s were years of hope and expectation in the adult education world and there was disappointment when County Colleges 'went on to the official back burner'. But, at Queen Anne Street in the mid-1960s there was great enthusiasm for the rising stars of the short-term residential colleges as Joan Raymond's special *Reminiscence* tells. Graham Wilkinson quotes Sir Richard Livingstone, a distinguished Oxford scholar of the mid-century, titling his article about the colleges as

The lamp of wisdom still burns brightly. Graham is Principal of Alston Hall in succession to Brian Leighton, a college near Preston, which was opened by Sir Robert Adam, the first President of NIAE after the merger of BIAE and NFAE.

The tally of web-site entries includes Leicester University's public orator's citation of the conferring of a *Doctorate upon NIACE's first chief officer: Edward Moss Hutchinson.* The speaker for the occasion was Professor Arthur Humpherys.

Vibrant, changing and facing new challenges – words titling the last section on the web-site. Alan Tuckett offers a perspective of NIACE, the changes that it has necessarily made during the last decade of the 20th Century, and the challenges it faces in the years ahead. He expresses his conviction that NIACE today is a lively, strong and relevant organisation that looks forward to the 21st Century with great hope for the future of the learning passion among adults.

HOWARD GILBERT
Individual Member of NIACE

THE ORIGINS OF NIACE

LORD HALDANE; THE HALDANE TRUST; THE BRITISH INSTITUTE OF ADULT EDUCATION; AND SIR WILLIAM EMRYS WILLIAMS

Howard Gilbert

LORD HALDANE began the process. In 1921 a small group of people – mainly University teachers and administrators – joined with Haldane to found the BIAE. The initial membership had an upper limit of 600 individuals, in contrast to today's large institutional and individual support. Those who joined were employed, principally, in university liberal adult education, which was a central part of Government education policy stemming from the 1919 Report of the Ministry of Reconstruction (Great Britain, 1919). Haldane became the Institute's first President, and Honorary Life President soon after 1926 until his death in 1929. A memorial appeal was launched in the House of Lords to provide a trust fund that would help to sustain the Institute he had founded. The target was £100,000; however, only a little over £5,000 had been subscribed by 1934. It was a time of severe hardship, economic stringency and uncertainty, and 'short commons'. In that year, J.W. Brown, the fund Honorary Secretary, prepared a Trust Deed for the investment of the capital which specified that income, up to a maximum of £500 per annum, should be paid to the BIAE.

Three Trustees were appointed to serve for three years. To secure continuity the Deed provided that:

> on the occasion of the first appointment...Trustees shall be appointed for terms of one year, two years and three years respectively...and the income when paid was ...to be applied in

furtherance of the general objects and purposes to develop which the
said Institute was founded by Lord Haldane.

In 1951, by Order of the Board of Education, the annual income and capital were transferred to the NIAE, following its establishment through the
merger of the British Institute and the National Foundation (1949). When
the funds became due for re-investment in 1969, the Honorary Officers of
NIAE were authorised to be the new Trustees. The Haldane Memorial
Trust continues to contribute to NIACE's income: the fund is part of the
investment portfolio in the Annual Accounts.

The sole witness to Brown's signature in 1934, was William Emrys
Williams of 2 Kingsley Close, (London) N2, a neighbourhood close to
Hampstead Garden Suburb and, curiously – as may be apparent shortly –
just off Falloden Way. He was in his first year as BIAE Secretary and ulti-
mately to become celebrated in adult education, in the service of the War
Office (1940-45) and with the Arts Council of Great Britain.

Who was Lord Haldane (Viscount Haldane of Cloan in Scotland)?

He was born into an old Scottish family; one brother was Professor J. B. S.
Haldane of Imperial College, another – John Sanderson Haldane – was a
physiologist and geneticist. Haldane himself was a lawyer and philosopher. He became politically prominent from 1905 when appointed to
Government as Secretary for War, and remained so until his death.
Elected as Liberal MP for East Lothian in 1885 he relinquished his seat in
the Commons in 1911 on succession to the peerage. A diary note by Beatrice Webb, founder member of the Fabian Society and wife of Sidney
(later Lord Passfield), gives an insight into his character. She was a close
watcher of the political shifts and changes. On Haldane's appointment to
government she wrote:

The great coup is to get Haldane to take the War Office, the courtly
lawyer with a great capacity for dealing with men and affairs and a
real understanding of the function of the expert, and skill in using
him.

In the Asquith Government (1911-16) he was Lord Chancellor leaving office and the Liberal Party for Labour – in 1916, when Lloyd George became Prime Minister of a coalition. He returned as Lord Chancellor in 1924 in the brief Labour administration and, thereafter was Labour Leader in the House of Lords and an advocate of Lords Reform.

As War Minister, Haldane reformed the army administration, established the Officer Training Corps scheme for Public Schools, and organised an emergency army group, which became the British Expeditionary Force at the outbreak of the First World War in 1914. Sir Edward Grey (Grey of Falloden), also a Scot, and Foreign Minister from 1908 to 1916, was a friend for many years.

Haldane's interest in education seems to have grown from the roots of his own experience. He studied philosophy at Göttingen University, followed an MA course at Edinburgh, achieving First Class Honours (1876) and completed training as a lawyer at Lincolns Inn in 1879. At about this time he lectured at the Working Men's College in London. In law he specialised in Commonwealth cases, appeals to the Privy Council, and Scottish appeals to the House of Lords. His advocacy for the extension of university education beyond the boundaries of Oxford and Cambridge was lifelong. In 1898 he was a lead counsel for the London University Charter hearings, performing a similar role for Liverpool in 1902. Edinburgh elected him Lord Rector in 1905, and Bristol offered the Chancellorship in 1914. He served as Chairman of the University Grants Committee, and in 1918 was appointed to the same office on the Royal Commission for Education in Wales. He aided and Chaired the Council of Imperial College, South Kensington. He knew Dr.Thomas Jones, former Deputy Secretary to the Cabinet and, after 1930, Secretary of the Pilgrim Trust, who founded Coleg Harlech of which Haldane was President from 1927 to 1928. After his death his step-sister, Elizabeth, wrote:

> *Until his last illness, adult education and its various forms (university and non-university) continued to engross his attention, and he constantly spoke in its favour.*

Education policy was the reason for his departure from the Liberal Party in 1916 and, without doubt, his interest in extending opportunities for university education led him to found the British Institute of Adult Education in 1921. He had been President of Birkbeck College, London, from 1919 and continued to be so until 1928. Viscount Haldane of Cloan died on 19 August 1928.

The British Institute of Adult Education

In the same year the British Institute published its second *Handbook and Directory of Adult Education.* The Institute's own pages list its officers and council members. There are also details of the Committee that had responsibility for the Handbook itself. Political balance and high level support are two striking features. Sir John, later Lord Justice, Sankey was President; Vice-Presidents were, respectively, the Rt. Hon. Stanley Baldwin (Prime Minister – Conservative), Viscount Grey of Falloden (Liberal), and Rt.Hon. J. R. Clynes (Labour) and former Lord Privy Seal, in a few months to become Home Secretary. Chairman was Dr. Albert Mansbridge, and the Vice-Chairman, Professor Harold Laski (Advisor to the Labour Government of 1945-50). The Institute had both an Honorary Secretary, the Rt. Hon. Oliver Stanley (Conservative and, in the 1930s, destined to become successively: president of the Board of Education, and the Board of Trade), and a Secretary: Professor T. H. Searls.

The BIAE Council had 27 members, representatives of a variety of organisations with interests in the education of adults. Grace Hadow, Vice-Chairman of the WI and Denman College, but also Principal of Oxford Home Students (a women's network for those seeking university-level education but unable to enter full-time courses), was a member. This group was the embryo of what became St. Anne's College, Oxford. R. S. Lambert, from BBC Education, was another strong Institute supporter. He became a member of the Gramophone Committee (1932) advocating its wide use in education, and involved similarly in the Mechanical Aids to Learning Group (1931). He Chaired the Institute's enquiry into public reading habits in 1933. Others on the Council were Barbara Wooton, economist and Director of the London Tutorial Classes, G. D. H. Cole of the Tutor's Association, and Professor F. E Cavenagh of Swansea, and later, Kings College. Trades union interest was represented by Arthur Creech-Jones, Transport and General Workers Union (TGWU), and a representative from provincial universities was Professor Robert Peers from Nottingham. The *Handbook*'s Editor, was Dr. Basil Yeaxlee, a Council Member.

Several members of the Council and some from its Publications Group were also appointed to the Board of Education Adult Education Committee. The latter's term of reference have a remarkable, contemporary ring:

> *To promote the development of liberal education for adults... to bring together...(providers)...so as to ensure mutual help and prevent overlapping and waste of effort; to further the establishment of local voluntary organisations for the purpose and of arrangements for co-operation with Local Education Authorities; and to advise the Board... upon any matters which (it) might refer to the Committee.*

BIAE Council Committee members who served on the Board's Committee included, Grace Hadow, Revd. F.E. Hutchinson, Jenkin James, Albert Mansbridge, J.W. Muir, Robert Peers, Dr. Yeaxlee, and Sir Benjamin Gott, Secretary of Education, Middlesex County Council. The *Handbook* carries an article by Gott, in which he outlines the duty of a Local Education Authorities (LEA) towards the provision of adult education. In the NIAE 50th anniversary publication of its journal *Adult Education: Aims and action in adult education*, (1921-1971) (Vol.50), Sir William Houghton, Education Officer for the Inner London Education Authority (ILEA), discusses similar issues in his contribution *The LEAs' response and responsibility.*

The *Handbook* of 1928-29 contains advertisements, which also touch issues that have been, or still are prominent in post-compulsory education for adults. One, under a banner headline *The Privileges of Citizenship* gave information about the education opportunities for adults offered by the London County Council, through its various centres, and tells readers where to apply for a range of eighteen curriculum pamphlets free of charge. Another presents Birkbeck College, for mature students; women are catered for at Hillcroft (residential college) in Surbiton. Miss Florence Axten LRAM, offers to teach people how to listen to music; Foyles Book

Shop provides books for students and, rather eccentrically for our day, there is an advertisement for Rowntrees Cocoa. (I recall my mother advising us children that the latter was good for 'a sound night's sleep'! She did not mention its value for study or homework!) Dr. Basil Yeaxlee, Secretary to the Publication's Committee, Member of the Council, and also of the Government's Adult Education Committee, was the author of several books. One is entitled *Lifelong Learning*. Published in 1929, the cover flap has a short notice, which gives us an insight of how teachers and organisers viewed adult education as the time.

> *Personal culture is a lifelong undertaking. It does not end when schooldays are over. Very often it only seriously begins when we set out to earn a living. Can we find anywhere an interpreter and guide who will give us understanding in the mysteries and treasures of our new-found world? This is the question which the Adult Education Movement sets out to answer.*

Basil Yeaxley had also his own particular style of humour. He concludes the *Preface* to the *Handbook* with these words:

> *Beyond doubt many users of this book could have compiled it better than the Editor has done. Therefore let every user heap coals of fire upon the Editor's head by sending him criticisms, corrections, and suggestions, whatever they are and when ever they occur. B.A.Y.*

Surely, this too must be a continuing circumstance in 2001 for more than adult education!

W. E. Williams

W. E. Williams is noted elsewhere in this publication as a remarkable man (see article by Harold Marks) and something of a 'flamboyant figure'. He was Secretary of the British Institute from 1934 to 1945, and doubled that responsibility during the War (1939–45) with secondment to the War Office as Director of ABCA. He also directed (in an Honorary capacity throughout the War), the exhibitions arranged by the Institute with the aid of the CEMA, called *Art for the People*. Their scope and range has been described by Williams himself, in the 50th Anniversary journal *Adult*

Education. They were by that account remarkable and, undoubtedly, his major interest in the education of adults. In the article he says:

> *I was…Secretary of the Institute, and my pre-occupation with the arts was not discouraged, (nor for that matter particularly encouraged) by a Council composed mainly of traditional representatives of the adult education 'establishment'. So the opportunity existed for me to propose an experiment in the diffusion of visual art.*

The exhibitions, featuring pictures (French and English art of the 19th and 20th centuries) loaned by private collectors, were very successful and became a major activity for the Institute pre-war, and, backed by Government and Pilgrim Trust funding provided and channelled through CEMA, throughout the period from 1940 to 1945. Williams was the major *animateur* in all the three organisations involved. The record, which is in some respects sketched in his article, suggests a certain blurring of function between them during the war-time operation. The Institute, for example, was instrumental in creating reading areas in the London air-raid shelters. Penguin Books, a venture in which Williams had editorial responsibilities from 1935 until 1963, donated 50,000 books for the shelter reading facilities.

However, the Institute was also involved in book provision for the troops, whilst ABCA and the Institute co-operated in encouraging the establishment of Army Study Centres, towards the end of the war. Funds to meet many of these activities came from the Pilgrim Trust, which also funded *Art of the People*, and its development over the same period of time. CEMA's founder members were Dr. Thomas Jones CH, Miss Thelma Cazalet MP, Sir Walford Davies, L du Garde Peach (playwright), Sir Kenneth Clark, and W.E. Williams. These constituted the Committee set up within the Institute to make proposals (to the Ministry of Information and the Board of Education) for the war-time development of 'informal' and 'practical adult education'.

The Pilgrim Trust provided £25,000 for the purpose, and the Government another £50,000. *Art for the People* became a central part of his project. Williams wrote (1971):

*With the aid of substantial funds from CEMA the Institute was able
to enlarge its activities considerably. In 1941 several new types of
exhibition were circulated. And the total of recorded attendances at
the major exhibitions was 367,000.*

He notes also that, under his Directorship of ABCA, study and information centres had been set up and 'Many were suitable for holding exhibitions …the Army (and later the Navy and the RAF) became ardent
customers of *Art for the People*'.

W.E. Williams left the British Institute in 1945 to become the peace-
time Director of the Bureau of Current Affairs (BCA), the civilian extension of the highly successful military services' scheme. The idea was to
provide a focus for education about political and social affairs, in a non-
partisan context, enabling the civil population and the returning service-
men and women, to re-establish themselves in civilian life ("civvie street"
was the current term). As Harold Marks says, of this essentially adult education experiment, 'it sadly disappointed in the long run', and ended in
1951. However, in the same time-span, Williams had become – in a voluntary capacity – Chairman of the Art Panel of the Arts Council, while the
British Institute appointed a new Secretary (David Wiseman) and from
1946 entered discussions with NFAE, with the idea of merging their
respective interests. In a contribution for this publication Wiseman comments that he was impatient for it (BAIE) to join forces with the National
Foundation because the Institute 'lacked the financial backing to remain
an independent body'. As is apparent from the evidence, this was the case:
much of the BIAE activity during the war had been financed with the
help of the Pilgrim Trust – the main funder with Government of *Art for
the People*. That source of revenue appears to have been significantly
reduced in 1945; one issue for the merger discussions was the future of *Art
for the People*.

Discussions between the merging bodies resulted in a representative
delegation meeting with Arts Council officers, W.E. Williams, Miss Glasgow (Secretary General) and Phillip James (Art Director to the Council).
It was agreed to recommend that the Arts Council assume responsibility
for *Art for the People*, which by this time had widened its function and
purpose considerably. Exhibitions were planned covering the design of

everyday things, to present various forms of architecture, and – what Williams describes as variants – occasions when artists were present to demonstrate. The war period had produced the competitions for art students. A variant was *Art by the People* in which paintings by local artists and art groups were featured. The Arts Council approved the recommendation, as did the Council of the British Institute. In his report back to that body, the BIAE's Chairman – A.C. Cameron – commented upon the 'spirit of co-operation and fairness shown by the representatives of the National Foundation', amongst whom was their Secretary, Edward Hutchinson.

A contemporary professional, the Education Secretary of the ECA, Harold Marks, later Staff Inspector for Adult Education at the Department of Education and Science (DES), has attributed to W. E. Williams some measure of influence in the shaping of the Butler Education Act 1944, in its clauses permitting arrangements for the education of adults. Marks was elected to the Institute's Council in 1947 and was present at the final meeting of that body before its merger with the National Foundation in 1949. At the conference, which sealed the jointure, a principal speaker was Professor F.A. Cavenagh who had been a BIAE member in its formative years following Lord Haldane's death. He urged the delegates to support the merger in which Edward Hutchinson, became Secretary, and David Wiseman, Deputy Secretary, of the newly established NIAE.

What, thereafter, of W.E. Williams?

In 1946 he had received the CBE for his wartime services. As already noted he was invited to Chair the Art Panel of the Arts Council. In 1951 he was appointed Secretary-General in succession to Miss Glasgow, and continued in that office until his retirement in 1963 at the age of 66. Throughout his career he had maintained an editorial association with Penguin Books and served for many years as its Editor-in-Chief.

He was an important witness in the case for the uncensored publication of *Lady Chatterley's Lover*, that caused such a sensation when printed by Penguin Books. His papers and letters about this are in the care of Bristol University Library. Sir Kenneth Clark, who had been one of the founders of CEMA in 1940, and appears to have been a lifelong friend, became Chairman of the Council in 1953. The two seem to have had a close working relationships, although one contemporary (David Piper) wrote that for Clark, the Chair – which he occupied until 1960 – was a 'frustrating experience'. He felt that he was little more then a 'figure-head.' Whatever the truth, when Clark, (now Lord) left the Chair in 1960, William's wrote in fulsome terms to him expressing regret at his departure.

April 29 1960

My dear K,
... The Arts Council had the luck to have you in the Chair during what, I am sure were the trickiest seven years of its adolescence, and your successors will find their work all the easier for what you have done for us, in that time. But that's not what I began to write about. I wanted simply to thank you for those years of friendship and gaiety and achievement. I shall never have it so good again.
As ever,
Bill

The two men maintained contact by letter and occasional meeting during the next 17 years.

He wrote to Clark shortly before he left the Council going into retirement. The letter is again over complimentary but expresses also, the uncertainty common to many a senior person facing imminent retirement:

21 January 1963

My dear K,
I was very sorry to hear I had missed you when you dropped in last Thursday. All the more so because 24 hours earlier I had read some words of yours which moved me very deeply indeed. I can't tell you how proud I am of that Ruskin dedication. You have done me innumerable generosities in all these years, but nothing more acceptable than this. If I live to be 90 as I hope I shall, I'll take down your Ruskin from the shelf nearest the fireplace and read that piece out to the District Nurse who will have come in to make my gruel.

I am getting ready to leave here now (The Arts Council) and am very willing to go. I've joined the Times already and must soon choose between pleasant offers from the Observer and the Sunday Telegraph. I've also got some books to write. But I don't want to be over-committed to writing, and I hope that I'll get a part-time stint or two in some practical activity. Everyone says 'O you'll be all right', but as clock and calendar move on one gets an occasional cold sweat!

My love to you both,

Bill

Sir William Emrys Williams, CBE, Hon.D.Litt, retired shortly after this was written. He became part-time Secretary of the National Art Collections Fund, until 1970. He was radio critic for the Observer and TV critic for the New Statesman. During the 1970s he, and Gertrude (née Rosenblum), and former Professor of Social Economics at London University – awarded the CBE in 1963 – went to live at Haddenham near Aylesbury. In a letter to Clark in May 1975 he says that his autobiography, which he has been commissioned to write, proceeds at a 'snail's pace', because his heart isn't in it. However, he ends on a more positive note:

I am enjoying the pastimes of a septuagenarian – sitting by my pond, in this lovely, vivid garden and larking about with the funniest black spaniel on earth.

A year later, in another letter responding to one received, he confesses to missing London life and then adds:

… I shall be 80, if I have another birthday. As one J.M. Synge's characters said, in the incommunicable accent & rhythm 'No man at-all can be livin' for ever, and we must be satisfied.

He was born at Capel Isaac's, Carmarthenshire, on 5 October 1896, to Annie and Thomas Owen Williams. His father was a journeyman joiner; he was the only son, had three sisters – two of whom died young. The family moved to Manchester when he was aged eight, where he went to school, and onto Manchester University. He, and his wife, were graduates of the University – she gaining a first class honours degree in Political Science and Economics. Both came to London. She to employment in the

University, and ultimately Professor of Social Economics; awarded a CBE; he to the post of Tutor in the Extra-Mural Studies Department, specialising in English Literature – an unpopular subject at the time. William Emrys Williams died on 31 March 1977.

Sources

Adult Education, Vol 50, No 4

A History of Modern British Adult Education, Fieldhouse, R. (1996) Leicester, NIACE

BIAE *Minutes* of 1946–48 and 1934–38

British Institute of Adult Education *Annual Reports* 1939, 1940, 1941, 1942, 1943, 1944, 1945

British Institute of Adult Education, *Second Handbook of the BIAE,* 1928–1929, (ed) Yeaxlee B. A.

Coleg Harlech Anniversary Publication 1930/1950

Dictionary of National Biography

Education of Adults in Britain

Haldane Memorial Trust Deed

Letters of W E Williams in the Arts Council Archive, V & A Museum

NIACE Archive

Our Partnership (Beatrice Webb)

Howard Gilbert

Howard Gilbert is an Individual Member of NIACE, and a former Council and Executive member. He was elected by the Individual Members' meeting to research and prepare this publication celebrating the 80th Anniversary of NIACE.

FUSION NOT FISSION

THE BIAE SECRETARY REMEMBERS

David Wiseman

I WAS APPOINTED Secretary of the BIAE at the end of 1946. I'd had a couple of years' experience in adult education after coming down from University in 1938 and had served six years in the army in Africa, the Middle East and Germany. This hardly fitted me to take over the reins of the British Institute or to follow in the steps of my predecessor, W.E.Williams.

It became obvious to me very quickly – and must have been obvious to my Council – that the NFAE was filling many of the purposes for which the Institute was founded. The Foundation was soundly based financially, the Institute less so.

One of the Institute's (BIAE) main activities was the publication of *Adult Education*, which made a significant contribution to the movement's thinking. It had had a succession of notable men as its editor. Editing it became one of my responsibilities, a part of my work, which was close to my heart.

Perhaps the Institute's most popular activity was the holding of a conference at an Oxford College each summer. To these conferences came many Directors of Education and others active in the service. They were drawn partly by the opportunity to relax in the quiet of academe, but mainly to participate in discussions of important themes free of administrative pressures and the nuts and bolts of management. Some of the liveliest minds of the time were invited to address the conference, Lord David Cecil, Elizabeth Bowen, A.J.P.Taylor, among others. And I remember, with singular pleasure, the skilled and modest chairing of one conference by Jack Longland, Director of Education for Derbyshire. These were rare and satisfying occasions and nothing comparable has succeeded it.

Another function the Institute performed was a consequence of one of W.E.Williams's innovations. I'm not sure what part he played in the establishment of CEMA, (which later became the Arts Council) but at the Institute we had responsibility for the compilation and distribution of exhibitions *Art for the People*. As a result museum directors and artists were frequent visitors to Tavistock Square, where we had our headquarters.

The Institute had the nucleus of a good library of material on the history of adult education. This was transferred to the National Institute.

However interesting the work of the BIAE, it lacked the financial backing to remain an independent body. I was impatient for it to join forces with the National Foundation. I knew that Edward Hutchinson, the hard-headed, ambitious and capable Secretary of the Foundation, had a far better claim than I to be in charge of whatever body came into being as a result of the fusion. In the event, I became Deputy Secretary and Publications Officer of the new National Institute, but had no intention of remaining and began looking for other openings. I resigned in September 1950 on my appointment as a Lecturer at the University College of the Gold Coast. But that's another story.

David Wiseman

David Wiseman was Secretary of the British Institute (BIAE) until 1949 when it 'fused' with the National Federation for Adult Education to form NIAE, with Edward Hutchinson at its head. On his return from the Gold Coast, David went to teach and become headmaster in Cornwall. He writes books for children and is now retired. This marks his first contact with the Institute since he left in 1950.

REMINISCENCES CONCERNING NIACE AND ITS PREDECESSORS

Derek Legge

French leave? A Regimental Sergeant Major's eventful two days

1943

'Attended the BIAE Conference called to discuss the Government's proposals for the post-war shape of British education, including the education of adults. It was held at the City Literary Institute (the City Lit. today), in Stukeley Street, just off Drury Lane, London.

I took two days off from the army – fairly easy for a Regimental Sergeant Major to do! We met on Friday 29 October, 5.00pm to 8.30pm and on Saturday 30 October, 9.30am to 5.30pm. Conference fee: 5 shillings (25 pence today!).

I remember meeting committed senior adult educators of the day, and other sympathisers, e.g. Henry Morris, Barbara Ward, T. G. Williams as well as W.E. Williams, the then Director of ABCA and – technically – Honorary Secretary of the BIAE, although on secondment to the War Office.

All were Individual Members of the Institute – this was their organisational basis – although many came from bodies connected with the service provision, or from LEAs which had asked them to attend. The general commitment was to the ideas of liberal adult education.

The opening address was given by Professor E. A. Cavenagh on *The White Paper and Adult Education.* Cavenagh had been my tutor when I trained as a teacher at King's College, University of London (Teacher's

Diploma). The White Paper was, of course, the prelude to the 1944 Education Act prepared by R. A. Butler, then President of the Board of Education.

There was a record attendance of over 270 people."

'I saw it happen ... The birth of NIAE'

1949

"Conference at Buxton – officially the second conference of NFAE established three years earlier.

This conference saw the coming together of the BIAE and the NFAE to form the NIAE. Memory suggests that it was difficult to tell the differences between members of the two organisations and the conferences. There was considerable common membership. As an Individual Member of the BIAE, I went to this NFAE conference representing the Tutors' Association.

I remember meeting Venables, as well as other leaders, and developing lasting friendships. Meetings were in the Pavilion which allowed for informal chats. There was a good address by Sir John Maud, then Permanent Secretary of the (newly created) Ministry of Education."

Background notes
Pre-war BIAE conferences had been held usually at either Oxford or Cambridge; this was the first since the outbreak of war in 1939, and the first time in London. The City Lit was 'brand new' – the pride of the London County Council which, almost since the foundation of the BIAE in 1921, had a forward-looking policy towards the provision of liberal adult education.

Henry Morris was Secretary for Education in Cambridgeshire and whose village college programme (the attempt to negate rural decline by establishing community lifelong learning centres) was being reviewed in the context of possible post-war developments. Four, including Sawston – the first – had been constructed before 1939.

Others present were T. G. Williams, Principal of the prestigious Institute in which we were meeting; Barbara Ward the economist, and W. E. Williams – mentioned above, but destined to become Secretary General of the Arts Council, 1951.

Derek Legge, at the time of the conference, was responsible for the education of troops manning anti-aircraft batteries throughout Greater London. He did so, travelling to each from his HQ on a motor cycle.

Derek Legge

Derek Legge MBE is an Honorary Life Member of NIACE and received his public honour for lifelong services to adult education. He was Head of the Department for Adult Education at Manchester University and, as his reminiscence notes show, he has been closely connected with the 'Movement' since the early days of the founding of NIACE. These short vignettes are drawn from his personal, extensive collection of records and his library.

THE BEGINNING OF THE NATIONAL INSTITUTE OF ADULT EDUCATION

Henry Arthur Jones

M Y APPRENTICESHIP in adult education (as it used to be called in palaeoscriptural times) was served under Ross Waller at Manchester. His commitment to the ancient liberal traditions made him (despite an inborn aversion from any sort of organisation) sympathetic to the old BIAE and it was from him that I learnt about it. Then, under his influence, I graduated from part-time to full-time work, as Resident Tutor for Northwest Derbyshire in the Manchester University Extra-Mural Department. That was in January 1947.

Buxton was in my parish, and Buxton happened to be chosen, two years later (1949), as the location for '*a conference*'. So I was nominated to attend as the representative of Manchester University. What I didn't know but soon came to suspect, was that this nomination, of the rawest and most junior of the University's personnel, was intended to be read as an insult, or at least a brush-off. For this was the occasion when the NIAE was born, though it was described at the time not as a Nativity but a Nuptial. The old British Institute had been dominated by the Responsible Bodies – the WEA, the ECA, certain other voluntary bodies, and the University Extra-Mural Departments – which were sustained by direct grant from the Ministry of Education.

For reasons to do with the grandeur thought to have been conferred on LEAs by the 1944 Education Act, this situation was resented by the LEAs as anomalous and a plot was hatched soon after to regularise it. In this the central figure was, I believe, William (later Sir William) Alexander of the Council of Local Education Authorities. The idea was to set up a new body, the NFAE, whose purpose would be to negotiate directly with government for all grants to adult education, supplement them with LEA funds, and then distribute the total among the various providers.

It was duly set up in 1946, a typical administrator's Big Idea: totally impractical, and within a year it was seen to be so. Now, therefore, it was to be supplanted by an even newer body. The Foundation was to be combined with the old British Institute to form the NIAE. This Conference was to be the occasion.

Flowing around all this was what sailors call 'funny water' – eddies and underwater currents, whirlpools and cross-flows – that a rookie like me found utterly fascinating. Ernest Green, General Secretary of the WEA, was warmly in favour of the Foundation idea, as he was at pains to explain to me. At present, he said, when each Responsible Body negotiates its own grant, the result is a feeble process in which government can divide and rule. Centralisation would bring immeasurable strength.

On the other hand the WEA District Secretaries were openly hostile and the extra-mural directors had indicated their indifference by generally ignoring the invitation to the Conference. But Chief Education Officers were there in abundance.

If there was much of a formal agenda, I cannot recall it. The main business was a pre-arranged (or as we say, spin-doctored) 'consultation' about the merger of the BIAE with the Foundation to form the new NIAE. This was presented as a marriage in which all would live happily ever after. There were the inevitable best-man jokes about marriages. The Director of Education for Tottenham (yes, that shows how long ago it was) made an urbane and witty bride's-father speech, which had everything but content. The Director of Education for Manchester, gave one of his characteristic three-sentences-per-paragraph speeches: two sentences of prose followed by a recondite quotation – what was once described as 'his star-spangled manner'.

The centre-piece, however, was a long soliloquy by Bill Alexander, opening with a Scotsman's joke which I remember clearly: two men out fishing in a small boat whose only heater was a bottle of whisky, were overtaken by fierce weather. In extremes one turned to prayer: 'O God, bring us safely out of this and I'll never touch another drop...' But the words stuck in his throat. A second and third attempt ended likewise, but then his companion whispered, 'dinna commit yourself. I think it's clearing.' This was greeted with laughter and applause. I was puzzled as to what this assembly of eminent educationlists was applauding. The manner of the telling? Or the advice never to commit oneself?

None of the speeches displayed the slightest doubt that the union was about to take place. Clearly we were all committed to that. There was no mention of the staff of the BIAE, or of its officers; and the National Foundation was quietly buried, as is customary, I suppose, with foundations.

Hovering around all these proceedings was a tall, slightly stooping figure, handing out bits of paper like an invigilator, occasionally bending over the chairman to drop a word in his ear. He remained mysterious until the end of the business when he was introduced as Edward Hutchinson, Secretary-Designate of the new Institute. A whispered query to my neighbour told me that he was Deputy Treasurer of Surrey County Council and on the Council of London WEA District.

When the introduction was made, Edward was invited to say a few words. I cannot recall exactly what he said, but it was something like: 'I promise to do my best in the job. May I remind delegates to check out at Reception and settle any outstanding accounts before leaving?' It seemed clear from this appointment that the new Institute was expected to follow a different line from that of the old one.

Edward Hutchinson, an economist and accountant, seemed to me at the time an unlikely successor. In fact he turned out to be an inspired choice (to the surprise, I still believe, of those who appointed him). He certainly had not listened to Alexander: no one was ever more committed to the cause of adult education. Immensely hard-working, practised in the ways of Whitehall and Council Offices, stimulating in discussion but hard-nosed in judgement, he went on to establish the Queen Anne Street office as a welcoming centre for adult-educators of all sorts, with a growing library and a firm concern for research and publication. He also understood money. The joke among friends was that the Institute's resources were husbanded by him: that is, he treated them like a working-man's wage packet – never let the wife know how much is in it, give her what's needed but reluctantly and with due deliberation.

When Brian Groombridge became Deputy Secretary they made an ideal pairing: Brian with his imaginative and innovative mind (ironically bringing forward much of the ethos of the old British Institute); Edward with his feet firmly on the ground of the possible; and both of them with a passionate faith in the cause they served.

NIAE at this time became a co-ordinating and campaigning body, promoting co-operation between the voluntary agencies and the increasingly involved local authorities. It also engaged energetically with central government. But it never became identified with any sector; it was always sturdily independent. One result was that when the Russell Committee was set up in 1968, Hutchinson was left out. A somewhat petty Whitehall revenge that wounded him deeply – not from personal pique but because he believed, rightly, that his experience, and especially his international connections and experience, could be valuable to the Committee.

Working closely with the Institute staff in later years, I often found myself recalling that Buxton arranged marriage. 'Dinna commit yourself'. There had been rhetoric their but no vision. It all seemed to me so bloodless, so emptily political, so remote from the energy and enthusiasm of the people I met in my classes, that I could not help seeing it as the making of a box in which adult education could be shut tidily away lest it become disturbing. And the Secretary-Designate, that sober, book-keeping local government officer, soft-shoeing among the delegates, seemed such a safe choice for them. What a misjudgement was that!

Never fail to take seriously a serious man.

Henry Arthur Jones

(Henry) Arthur Jones is Emeritus Professor at the University of Leicester, and previously its Vice-Chancellor. A strong supporter of the Institute when Principal of the City Lit., he was a long time friend of Edward Hutchinson and his wife. He is an Honorary Life Member of NIACE, and a former Executive Committee Chairman.

AN INSPECTOR RECALLS THOSE EARLY YEARS

Harold Marks

REFLECTING ON MY early connections from 1946 to 1950 in particular with the then NFAE, I am particularly struck by the modest scale of the operation as run for a long time by Edward Hutchinson, and its relatively remarkable effectiveness. Like the BIAE, it was really a one-man show, backed up by powerful concerned academic establishment figures.

W.E.Williams's contribution through the British Institute was remarkable both for its width and its effectiveness. As Secretary (1934–45), working only with a personal assistant, (the redoubtable Miss Katherine Chick), as well as pressing for the development of the range of provision included in the capital-letter-headed Adult Education title, and latterly for its inclusion in the 1944 Education Act, he had much peripheral influence. He helped with the early development of a broadcasting adult education contribution, and his interest in the popularisation of the Arts led to the foundation of CEMA and its progeny the Arts Council, of which he later became Secretary-General. He also was active in the development of popular cheap serious publishing with Pelican Books.

A further major initiative in ABCA[1] had great if sometimes politically exaggerated adult education contemporary influence though it sadly disappointed in the longer run. Perhaps Williams bore some responsibility for this in the scale of the attempted post-war civilian continuing model, which somehow fitted the rather flamboyant figure I recall at an early

---

1   The Army Bureau of Current Affairs whose style and activity was modelled upon lines consonant with liberal adult education (with modifications to suit military circumstances). A civilian continuation was developed (BCA) but failed in 1951.

NIACE conference. My now aged thinking, concerned characteristically often with "might have beens", may speculate on the possible but unrealised influence which its survival and development might have had on adult education as a politico-social educational force, modifying its erosion towards cultural educational concerns almost exclusively only, however valuable these have been in themselves and in the enormously widening constituency they attracted, before this was restricted to the relatively well-off.

The main reason for the failure in the early post-war years to secure the anticipated significant expansion of adult education lay of course in the shortage of available public funding. Coming himself from the job of a treasurer in local government with a voluntary interest in the WEA, Edward Hutchinson saw the importance of appealing to and working closely with the Local Authorities and from the beginning recognised the financial advantage of linking the new Institute closely with them. Whether in doing this he foresaw a likely continuing lack of high level central departmental concern for adult education among all the claimant calls on its resources, may be ascertainable from NIACE records; it is certain in retrospect that the development of adult education achieved in the following four decades gained enormously from his recognition of the possible central role of the LEA associations and some if not – despite his continuing efforts – all LEAs as major providers, until central government developed its new restrictive adult education policy in the 1980s.

Edward continued in the NIAE the modest structure that characterised the tradition of the British Institute. Almost as a 'one-man band' he edited *Adult Education*, which was for years effectively almost the sole publication helping those concerned with the area. He developed the Institute as the main and for long the only active focus of academic and practical thinking about adult education, and also carried through significant research, as well as organising an Annual Conference which brought together the gradually increasing number of interested and active practitioners with the providing bodies. This he did in addition to influencing development by personal contact and what has become known, I think, as networking, together with running an administrative machine and its Executive Committee and widely representative Council.

Generally I found Council meetings, to which I went to from time to time, formal and dull, and as a member of HM Inspectorate concerned with adult and community education I got less out of the Annual conferences than those who did not have our opportunity of seeing so much of the variety of provision on the ground. Edward rightly was charitably critical of us for not making our knowledge more widely available for public use, though he valued much HMI opinion and advice and understood their problems. The Conference which sticks in my memory is one at which the Minister, at the polite and formal dinner which always was part of the proceedings, was roundly as well as politely but effectively denounced for the failures of government policy then becoming more fiercely restrictive of adult education. But in Edward's day, and doubtless still, the general influence of the NIACE on policy and provision was more discretely and often fortunately more effectively exercised.

Editor's note

A wide-ranging exposition of the post-war work of HMI, in adult education and related disciplines, apart from provision in further education colleges, has been published recently by NIACE. Under the title *An education for the people?* Konrad Elsdon and others discuss the ways – diverse and devious on occasion – by which the small 'Other Further Education' inspectorate (and its successors) sought to achieve a significant place for adult education between 1944 and 1992. Harold Marks contributes to several Chapters 'particularly and largely' including that upon Adult Education. ISBN 1 86201 100 9. NIACE 2001.

Harold Marks

Harold Marks was Staff Inspector for Adult Education at the Department of Education and Science. He became a member of the British Institute's Executive Committee a year before its amalgamation with the National Federation for Adult Education. He was then Education Secretary for the Educational Centres Association.

CHEFS IN A HOT KITCHEN

RECOLLECTIONS OF
EDWARD HUTCHINSON:
MENTOR AND FAMILY FRIEND

Saskia Heasman

M Y MEMORIES OF Edward Hutchinson go back to my earliest childhood, as my parents knew him before I was born. Towards the end of the Second World War, Edward was living alone in Surrey, in a flat, while Enid and the children were evacuated to the Lakes. He advertised for a couple to live in the flat with him, sharing the expenses and for the wife to do the cooking and cleaning, etc. My parents who were bombed out six times in the War had just been bombed out again, answered the advertisement and were accepted. Thus began a friendship which was to last for the rest of Enid's and Edward's lives.

When Enid returned and my parents left to set up their own home we all became family friends, seeing each other fairly often. When the Hutchinsons were moving from Cheam to Richmond in the early fifties, Edward's eldest son Martin stayed with us for a few months while continuing his studies at medical school. Consequently, unlike most of my contemporaries, I had actually heard of 'adult education' while I was still at school myself.

It was entirely due to Edward and Enid that I eventually went into adult education, because I spent my last term at school with them in 1964, my parents having moved from North London to Reading. During that time, I attended my first adult education class, Spanish, at the City Lit. I had studied Spanish from nothing to 'A' Level in two years, so I needed all the help I could get! Another memory of that time is Edward offering to give me a reference if I ever wanted a job as a cook   I must have cooked a successful meal that day!

Three years later, I did my PGCE at Maria Grey College, in Twickenham, and lodged with friends of the Hutchinson's in Kew, so I saw Edward and Enid fairly often and joined another City Lit class, this time Advanced Linguistics, which I really enjoyed. So it is not really surprising that I subsequently decided to first, teach evening classes in addition to my day-job in a school, but later to run an evening centre, and eventually to do a Diploma in Adult Education at Nottingham University, at Edward's suggestion as then being the best place to do the course. I made use of my contacts and arranged for Edward, who by then had retired from NIACE, to come up and give us a presentation as part of one of my pieces of work on the course.

I have worked with adults ever since, and I am convinced that it is all due to knowing the Hutchinsons. I have to say that I have never regretted it – I still get a buzz when I start a new year with a new group of students.

Saskia Heasman (née Saskia Mills)

Saskia Heasman knew Edward Hutchinson when she was a child. She is now partly retired but continues to teach adults part-time. Previously she was Adult Education Organiser at the Newark and Sherwood College in Nottinghamshire.

EDWARD HUTCHINSON

SECRETARY, 1949–1971

Brian Groombridge

EDWARD HUTCHINSON was the first Secretary as the Director was then called, of the NIAE. There was no certainty in those days that this good idea – the merged BIAE and NFAE – would succeed. To lead it someone was needed with a conceptual grasp of the unifying factors underlying all its work; who made no hierarchical distinctions of worth between the different partners in membership; who had the ability to make the case in speech and print for adult education in its various forms; and was preferably a good manager. That was not all; it was also desirable that the Secretary should be financially knowledgeable and astute.

Edward Hutchinson was, exceptionally, such a person. During the past 20 years or so, 'the accountants are in charge' has been a handy critical quip against the BBC and other public bodies; yet an accountant is just what Edward had been – but eminently one with vision, who understood and articulated the mission as well as the balance sheet.

Edward had been Deputy Treasurer, Surrey County Council, a 'reserved occupation' during the Second World War, requiring exemption from military service. He left this secure post after the war to take on the Institute. His wife Enid backed him, knowing the risk he was running, but the new organisation took root and he made it grow. Why did he want the job?

Edward's wish to work for the Institute and his lifelong commitment to it was grounded in his own experience. He was born in Penwortham, Preston, in 1909; left school at 14, working to support his recently widowed mother. He was in a dreary private business as an office boy/clerk for a few months, but then got a job as a clerk with Lancashire County Council. He studied the hard way with the WEA, at local authority evening classes, and by correspondence. He qualified as an Associate of the Chartered Institute of Municipal Treasurers and Accountants, and gained a mature scholarship from Lancashire Education Committee (£30 for 'composition fees' and travel). That enabled him to become an evening student at the University of Manchester (60 miles there and back), graduating as a BA (Admin). He wrote an MA thesis on local government (1937) and worked in local government finance until giving up his job with Surrey County Council in 1946.

An important early influence was a WEA economics tutor, Edward (Ted) Parkinson (later an adult education HMI). When Edward himself had his own first experience of being a tutor, he was only 18 – 'impressed', as he put it, 'into taking a class in English in Preston gaol'. After graduating, he became a regular WEA tutor, and when he moved to Surrey, one of his classes (on the Beveridge Report, (1942)) went so well that a thriving WEA branch was built out of it. Towards the end of the war, he became Honorary Treasurer of the London District WEA and represented them on the Council of London University's Extra Mural Department. It was then that he began to feel 'a desire to commit myself wholly to educational work', and made the major career move, taking on the challenging Institute job.

Edward started work for the Institute at 79 Wimpole Street; it had £700 in the bank, a second hand typewriter (£3) and a typist. After a few years, he and a small but growing staff moved to a suite of rooms at 35 Queen Anne Street (including a main meeting room, in which a good library from the previous regime was housed). Down the road (at No 12) were the headquarters of the Association of Education Committees (the Education Committees had their own national organisation, distinct from their local councils), whose pugnacious Scottish Director (Bill, later Sir William, later Lord, Alexander) was the Institute's first Honorary Treasurer and from then on an influential ally.

The Institute staff when I was first there consisted of Edward, an administrative secretary (Joan Carmichel), Edward's secretary (Grace Atkin), and an assistant for me. Yet it is not an exaggeration to say that almost from the start, and allowing for very big differences of scale, intensity, and frequency the NIAE performed then all the main functions that it performs now, largely because of its Director's unusual combination of qualities and skills. To use current NIACE job titles: as well as being Director, he was his own Finance Officer, Conference Manager, Information Systems Manager, Research and Development Officer, and Publications Officer (Joy Groombridge – née Samuel – was the first specialist in one of those roles, in charge of publishing for the Institute).

Though they often had to meet the subscription out of tight, reducing budgets, Edward regularly persuaded the institutional members that NIAE was worth belonging to. They included not only the universities and the WEA with their historic commitment to adult education, but a wide range of voluntary bodies and crucially, even the local education authorities, most of which had much ground to make up. He was also good at encouraging people to join (and to join in) as individual members.

Hence, though the staff was small, the work was shared with many others. A democratic constitution required that much of it was done by the officers and members of various committees. Edward enabled the partner organisations to understand that the Institute was their instrument. His hospitable manner and gift for friendship reinforced their representatives' sense of belonging.

Enough progress was soon made to expand the staff and take over an extra floor. The establishment was still small, with a few people doing laboriously what new technology does now. The tone was very much set by the Secretary. He led by example and inspired the staff to work hard. I particularly valued Edward's philosophical style: smoking cheroots (he gave them up as a health risk some time later), he would ask me and others to join him in his study while he thought aloud, articulating his latest ideas about this complex domain, discussing with us what needed to be done next to unify the field and make gains that would benefit people, society and democracy. Grace Atkin, who worked with Edward for much longer than anyone else (20 years in all), says the term 'employer' hardly seems appropriate: '…he was more a friend, guide and philosopher'.

Enid and Edward Hutchinson

This professional seriousness was matched by a relaxed and good-humoured regime. It was enjoyable as well as stimulating to work in Queen Anne Street. Everyone remarked on it – the many visitors from all over the world: temporary staff; and core staff. 'Edward generated loyalty, enthusiasm and team spirit,' Grace remembers: 'he was seldom inaccessible to his staff, and when there was pressure to get conference or meeting papers despatched; he would lead the lively and cheerful sessions around the library table.' Gill Bateman (née Leverton), a publications and administrative assistant, adds that everyone was willing to 'muck in' and Edward would mark staff birthdays and anything else remotely worth celebrating by producing a favourite wine (still a novelty for most of us at the time). He worked all hours, beyond the call of duty, though he did enjoy a brief siesta and we learned not to trouble him immediately after lunch.

Edward knew though that this was not a job to do done from a desk in London. He put himself about and became a familiar figure in different settings all over the country. Konrad Elsdon, an ECA Principal who became an HMI, puts it well.

Edward Hutchinson [took] a great deal of trouble to be out in the field, visiting institutions and individuals. As a result he had a good knowledge of any developments, of problem situations, and of people, regardless of seniority, who were thoughtful, effective or innovatory. He had a sure touch in identifying potential... in encouraging or even stimulating a piece of pioneering, or encouraging the young and shy to take the bit between their teeth – and then to write up the results in Adult Education. In this way he repeatedly acted as midwife to both major and minor research...or practical innovation – and to a good many careers. Some of the country's major ... projects owe much, or almost everything, to him. Yet he saw himself as the servant of adult education and unselfishly hid behind the results: Edward Hutchinson remained the Secretary of the Institute, but was respected nationally as presiding over what was in effect a learned body [and] an effective representative of a cause and a profession.

Elsdon remembers the work Edward did to make known Joe Trenaman's significant research on broadcasting and adult learning; I also recall how generously he supported Patrick Saul, who faced so many difficulties in setting up the British Institute of Recorded Sound (now the National Sound Archive, the pride of the British Library). He built bridges to related domains – for example, working with Peter Venables and others in technical education; he inspired the progressive report *Liberal Education in a Technical Age* (NIAE, 1955).

Edward was an acute observer of the political scene (soon after Margaret Thatcher came to power in 1979, he said to me, 'This is no ordinary Conservative administration: this is counter-revolution' (it was over a year before professional commentators began to notice the huge ideological shift she was achieving). His own views were essentially those of a radical. He used to say somewhat sharply that, 'the problem with the school system in Britain was that it was run by people who would never put their own children through it'. But as Secretary of the Institute he knew that the number of local authorities with a serious commitment to adult education – with lively programmes reaching people of all kinds, developed by professionally capable staff, in accommodation suitable for mature students – was a minority. They were in practice just as likely to be run by Tories as by Labour – Devon, for example, or East Sussex, Cambridge with its Village Colleges and other counties which signed up to 'the community use of community buildings', such as Leicestershire under Stewart Mason and his successor Andrew Fairbairn and Cumberland, as it was then, when Gordon Bessey was Director of Education.

There were indeed Conservative ministers with whom he had a good relationship, and Labour ones who made him restive. His political anger would be evident more publicly when yet another government (of either colour) sought to make significant savings in public expenditure by subjecting local authorities and others to another round of cuts in adult education. The motive could not be generally financial – and this was an accountant speaking – when 'the total amount spent on it was well within the margins of accounting error'

A keen internationalist, Edward was strongly committed to the Institute's international work. He was a close personal friend of the Dutch adult educator. 'Bob' Schouten, who with colleagues from France, Germany and Austria, created the European Bureau of Adult Education (EBAE) intended to foster a new, more democratic Europe. He served on the UK's UNESCO Commission, and was active in the International Council of Adult Education (ICAE). He was visiting professor at the Universities of British Columbia (1960), Syracuse (1969), and Liverpool (1971–72). He was awarded a rare honour from the French Government in1971 – *Chevalier dans l'Ordre des Palmes Académiques* – for services to Anglo-French relations and *education permanente*. This was a source of pride for him and his family. He was also delighted to receive honorary doctorates from the University of Leicester (1970) and the Open University (1982). The OBE (1964) was a bit of an embarrassment. He strongly disliked the hierarchical stress on titles in English public life, but it would have been a mistake for him, as the Institute's Director, to reject it (both his successors have been similarly decorated).

He was a prolific writer and an authoritative, thoughtful speech – maker. He expressed most of his ideas topically in the editorial *Commentary* in *Adult Education,* but never wrote a book about adult education as such. He co-authored two books with Enid Hutchinson stemming from her own groundbreaking projects in women's studies and access work. Unlike many men of his generation he was no male chauvinist, and his professional partnership with Enid was very important to him. At a time when the university departments, the WEA and the local education authorities were male-dominated, he shared her feminism; he was even a member of the Fawcett Society. It was due to his attitude and advocacy that the various women's organisations in membership of the Institute enjoyed their fellow members' respect and Edward's enthusiastic support.

There was only one Edward Hutchinson: there was not a public man and a quite different private one; he was all of a piece whether you met him at home, in his office or in conference. You could always rely on the same warmth, enthusiasm, dedication, reassuring competence and integrity. The current importance of NIACE obviously owes much to his two successors (Arthur Stock and Alan Tuckett) and to a host of other people, staff and member organisations, and passive representatives. But had it been mismanaged in those vulnerable, exploratory, early days, the Institute could have failed. They inherited a successful enterprise, enjoying national and international esteem, thanks to Edward's effective and idealistic leadership over many years.

Brian Groombridge

Brian Groombridge knew Edward Hutchinson nearly 40 years as employer, mentor, colleague, and friend. Brian was on the staff twice as a contract researcher, and later as Deputy Secretary. This tribute is adapted from Brian's forthcoming professional memoir 'Prospecting for a Democratic Society'

ARTHUR K. STOCK

DIRECTOR, 1971–1988

Paul Fordham

N<small>IACE HAS BEEN</small> lucky to have Directors well suited to their times and to the political climate in which they operated. Coming into the NIAE in the early 1970s, Arthur brought the vision of a 'big man' into an organisation which would need all the robust qualities that phrase suggests if it was not only to survive but even to prosper during the difficult years of the 1980s. It was Arthur who laid the two essential foundations for a different kind of growth in the late 1980s: the creation of various satellite units (e.g. REPLAN, UDACE) from which growth was possible, and beginning to move the basis of core funding away from almost total dependence on direct grants from DES and the LEAs. As the 1980s 'cuts' to adult education took hold, it would have been all too easy to sink back into the management of progressive decline rather than push ahead with the forward-looking stance which Arthur always brought to the job. The beginnings of the Government's REPLAN programme of education for unemployed adults illustrates the manner in which he always guided NIACE towards a positive agenda.

What started as a modest projects programme within REPLAN soon expanded into a much larger one, with NIACE eventually managing a nationwide team of Field Officer support. Under this management, it was never allowed simply to become a tool of Government. Arthur and his colleagues (notably Tony Uden) decided what elbow-room they had to promote a NIACE agenda as well as acting within (and continuing to influence) the policy parameters set by Government. There were difficult moments; but Arthur was both passionate and consistent in expressing

Arthur K. Stock

what he believed, and tough-minded enough in his advocacy to convince sceptical civil servants that he was right.

There was a moment when involvement in REPLAN almost slipped from our grasp. In 1983 senior civil servants had indicated they were 'minded' to let NIACE administer part of their new education programme for the adult unemployed. After much negotiation, and debate within NIACE, the question finally became whether or not NIACE would accept the money and on what terms: this was eventually debated at a special Council meeting in March 1984. In the view of both Arthur and myself, the expected outcome was that the Council would approve, as it did by a large majority – but first it was necessary that objectors should have the opportunity to give voice to their concerns.

Almost all the oral interventions were against, among them a suggestion that this was 'tainted' money because it was from a Government that had already cut funding to adult education. From the platform it was impossible to miss the look of alarm which crossed the face of the attending senior civil servant at the tone of these interventions; and we sensed we might be in trouble. It soon became apparent that we were right and that the DES was preparing not to involve NIACE in the way expected. Arthur at once asked for a meeting with DES to discuss this apparent *volte-face*.

The meeting was scheduled for 2.30pm, allowing enough time to explain a decision already taken but hardly enough to change it. However, to Arthur this was simply another challenge. Time was irrelevant in the face of his determination and commitment to ensure NIACE participation. The meeting went on until well after 7.00pm and might have gone on longer had there not been some vigorous foot contact under the table between Chairman and Director. But by then it was obvious that we had already won the argument. The DES would trust NIACE to deliver. On the whole it worked very well and the former internal critics on the NIACE Council were silenced. Eventually Government did shut down the programme, but only after seven years of successful intervention on behalf of unemployed adult learners.

In October 1980 the DES produced its discussion paper on *Continuing Education* (sub-titled *post-experience vocational provision for those in employment*: a signal if one were needed that the political climate was now radically different from the post-Russell years of the mid-1970s). Moreover, change in the political context was not simply a question of a change of government. Renewed emphasis on continuing (vocational) education had already been foreshadowed by Callaghan's Ruskin speech in 1976. Seven years later the changed emphasis in official thinking was complete. NIAE added the 'C' to its title in the same year (1983), to demonstrate that we were interested in the whole spectrum of provision. Arthur had to work out what this would mean in practice now that the election of Margaret Thatcher had reinforced the new emphasis.

A few months earlier (March 1980) in a pamphlet on *Adult Education in the United Kingdom* Arthur himself was still talking as if there would be a National Development Council along the lines recommended in the 1973 Russell Report. And he suggested that the existence of ACACE appointed in 1977 (under Richard Hoggart's chairmanship) meant that the Development Council was already 'partly established'.

Alas this was a dream not to be fulfilled. His later comment in the same paper was more prescient of what actually happened '...*to perceive the need for the change, to catch glimpses of the goals towards which changes should moving, but to... struggle to achieve the necessary changes without losing all continuity.*' Continuity came from his personal commitments and beliefs and his roots in LEA adult education: pushing for necessary changes from his inner drive and energy and from his sensitivity to the political context within which he worked.

His powers of expression, plus an unrivalled command of facts about the UK scene, meant that he could not only speak and write with great authority, but also advance an argument with convincing and detailed effectiveness.

Many of the ideas he tried to put into practice stemmed from his international interests; these helped reinforce already deeply held convictions regarding educational inequalities. In 1989 he recalled the importance of the ideas emanating from the third UNESCO World Conference in Tokyo (1972), which he attended soon after his appointment in 1971. Tokyo, he wrote, emphasised the 'forgotten people' who suffered from '*gross inequality in the distribution of knowledge and therefore of national, group and individual capability*' (Vol 61, 4, March 1989). No doubt there was also mutual influence and rapport between Arthur and that other 'big man' from the international scene, Roby Kidd, then in the process of establishing the ICAE. His interest in this and other international projects never wavered, though he was never captured by them and retained a healthy scepticism about their effectiveness. However, through these contracts, Arthur was able to supplement his unrivalled knowledge and understanding of the UK scene, with an ability to relate this to wider international trends (see Hall and Stock, 1985).

The passionate consistency referred to above contains at least two major themes and from these he would not be moved, either by forces of argument or in the interests of short-term political expediency. His equality agenda re-surfaced in various forms. If traditional provision by LEAs and the Universities was being cut then there had to be alternative ways of promoting it. He made sensitive responses to pressure groups representing women's interests, special needs, and ethnic minorities. Research was commissioned, committees were formed and, policies were changed. The current strong advocacy role of NIACE began to emerge under Arthur's leadership.

The other major theme was concerned with process. Arthur was always scathing about the 'front end' model of education so firmly embedded in the British official mind, even today. The idea that you only had to plan for an adequate system to 16+ or 18+ or some other terminal point was the kind of heresy he sought to expose on each and every occasion it arose. Of course the idea that adult education will always be necessary (however labelled) is one shared by all adult educators. But with Arthur it was a crusade from which he would not be turned aside. His strong support for the small Association for Recurrent Education throughout the whole of its life was one indication of how strongly he felt about this issue.

Arthur's directorship was marked by energetic action rather than the generation of new ideas. At the same time he provided the setting where new ideas could flourish, and he did not hesitate to draw on the corpus of 'old' ideas if this would ensure continuity. What mattered were the broader interests of adult learners as a whole. As well as supporting REPLAN he gave equally to its 'ideas' counterpart, UDACE. With the demise of ACACE and the failure of Government to agree to a Development Council, the creation of UDACE was widely seen as a conciliatory sop to the field, which was likely to be ineffective. Arthur's quiet support as well as the decided hard work of those appointed to staff it ensured that new ideas did emerge and that they were listened to by the Government.

When a new issue arose his first instinct was to consult the relevant field workers within and without the NIACE membership. For example, when the first REPLAN project money arrived, criteria had to be formulated in a great hurry to ensure rapid disbursement. DES officials needed guidance about what to do. It was Arthur who came up with proposals which ensured strong participation from field workers already working with unemployed adults, and this set the tone of the much bigger enterprise which was to follow under his Associate Director, Tony Uden, and later under his successor, Alan Tuckett.

As an administrator, Arthur was extremely well organised and worked hard to ensure the same exacting standards from others that he always set for himself. Budd Hall (Roby Kidd's successor as Director General of the ICAE) once remarked that whatever differences he might have had with Arthur he could always rely on a quick reply to letters and to invitations for joint action. He never forgot the idea of adult education as a 'movement', to support the poor, the 'forgotten', the under-educated, the excluded. And he helped keep that idea alive at a time when it would have been all too easy to downplay it.

The 'big man' enjoyed the strong support of his wife, Joyce Berney, as Publications Editor. She retained her own fierce independence, but their contribution was a real team effort. Together, with their passionate interests in skiing and sailing, they brought a breath of the energetic outdoors into NIACE, reminding us all that while professional dedication and hard work had to be a priority, there is also another life to be lived out there, preferably with equal passion and equal dedication.

Paul Fordham

Paul Fordham was Professor of Adult Education at the University of Southampton, and Chairman of the NIACE Executive Committee during some of the difficult times for the Institute in the 1980s. Throughout the time he successfully chaired the REPLAN project, working closely with Arthur Stock and Tony Uden, the programme manager.

ALAN TUCKETT

DIRECTOR, 1988–

Stephen McNair

I T I S I R O N I C that Alan Tuckett's first formal engagement with NIACE was through an initiative he had argued against. In 1983 at the Annual Conference in Guildford the Secretary of State, Sir Keith Joseph, announced the Government's intention to give NIACE a grant of £50,000 a year to set up a national development unit for adult education. Characteristically, Alan spoke for a small radical minority, with passion and style, arguing that the funding was inadequate, the strings would be too tight, and the interests of adult learners betrayed. But NIACE accepted the offer and UDACE was born. Two years later, its Steering Committee invited him to speak to its annual residential meeting. After he had gone one member commented, '*I may not know much about this field, but I know a good chap when I see one. We should get him on the Committee*', and we did so. He immediately began to play a very active role, applying intelligence, and powerful political skills to the work, and helping to steer the Unit through some controversial waters.

He brought an important range of experience to UDACE, and later to NIACE. As a student of literature at the University of East Anglia, when Malcolm Bradbury and Angus Wilson were establishing Creative Writing, he developed a literary style and range of reference which he applied as a powerful tool in speaking and writing. His work at the Brighton Friends Centre gave him a grounding in the paradoxical world where the liberal middle classes meet the world of radical social and educational thinking, which characterises much of the English voluntary sector. It was there that he launched the all-night teach in, and became a

Alan Tuckett

champion of student-centred learning in adult literacy, applying in practice some of the ideas of the radical theorists of the 1960s.

As a leading, if controversial, figure in ALRA and its successors he was one of those who fought for the view that literacy was as much about empowering learners to find their own voice, as about phonics and formal classes. It was these beliefs which took him into the International League of Social Commitment in Adult Education, a global gathering of radical adult educators which set out to challenge orthodoxies of many kinds, and which recognised his talents by electing him their President in 1986.

From the Friends Centre he went to ILEA, then by far the largest and best-funded adult education service in the country. As Principal of the Clapham and Battersea Institute he took on a large and complex role, demonstrating serious managerial skills, but without losing sight of the radical agenda. He became a prominent advocate for the service, honing his political skills and celebrating one of the great local authority adult education services with the benchmark document *The Jewel in the Crown (1988)*, as Government embarked on the abolition of the Authority. The alliances and skills from this period stood him in very good stead when he later began to raise the political profile of NIACE.

Despite this range of experience not everyone believed that he would be a "safe pair of hands" to take over the National Institute when Arthur Stock retired. Although NIACE had always, in its writing, endorsed a fairly radical agenda, Alan expected to apply it with rigour and enthusiasm, and he brought a number of dangerously unpredictable new ideas. He proposed to convert *Adult Education*, the worthy but rather staid house journal of the adult educators, into a large circulation national newspaper for adult students and staff. He also proposed to create a large-scale celebration of adult learning. Both seemed alarmingly risky. His senior colleagues advised against both, and were proved wrong. The significantly retitled journal *Adults Learning* did not become a mass circulation newspaper, but it did dramatically increase circulation and frequency, serving a much larger and more diverse audience than its predecessor. Adult Learners' Week became not only a tool for celebrating adult learning in all its diversity but, by linking individual learners directly to politicians, it lifted NIACE out of the box in which it had been contained for many years, relating to Government either through polite, friendly but marginal conversation with civil servants, or formally arguing in print with Ministers. Adult Learners' Week gave NIACE direct access to, and credibility with, Ministers and the wider policymaking community which proved invaluable as Government's interest in adult learning grew through the 1990s.

It also demonstrated Alan's ability to forge partnerships and alliances across a very wide range of agencies. The Week was never just a NIACE activity; it engaged all the broadcasters as no national educational initiative had ever done before, and it engaged providers and the world of business and industry, providing each with an opportunity to play to their own strengths and see the cause of adult learning as something which brought prestige and credit to their own organisations (and their individual careers). The power of the idea was demonstrated as it spread to other countries, and eventually UNESCO recognition.

When Alan became Director, NIACE was a small organisation. Its constituency was a long-standing community of adult educators, mainly from the liberal and non-vocational sectors. Government had, over a long period, failed to invest in the sector, and had deliberately chosen, when it did so, to put its money in separate agencies (ACACE), or into earmarked units like REPLAN and UDACE. As a result, despite the aspirations of its members, NIACE had become increasingly marginalised in the mainstream educational and political debates, carrying a torch for a radical theory but often with a cautious and conservative practice.

By the end of the 1990s, NIACE had become the centre of a web of relationships and initiatives built around the rapidly emerging lifelong learning agenda. It had grown spectacularly in influence, recognised around the world as one or the leading national organisations, and respected at home by Ministers and politicians of all parties, all proud to be associated with it. It had become the most serious publisher and conference organiser across a far wider field. It had grown in turnover and staff numbers, taking a well judged, but risky decision to move offices to provide more space to cope with growing workloads, and within five years was seeking more space as the building burst with staff and activity. It had extended its range of interests and ways of pursuing them, with new staff and kinds of staff, and new partnerships with other agencies. Alan's personal role had been recognised academically with a visiting Chair at Warwick University, and politically by the award of an OBE.

The personal and professional have always been closely linked in Alan's life. He met his wife, Toni Fazaeli, as a member of the interview panel when she joined UDACE as a Development Officer for Access. Their home in Leicester has been the resting place for many adult educators, travelling the world or just the UK. Their hospitality is warm and generous, and the birth of their son, Lewis, gave him the challenge of applying in practice the notion of NIACE as a family-friendly organisation. A feature of their wedding reception, held of course in an adult education college, was the speech from the bride, now an FE Inspector, presenting a rigorous analysis of the strengths and weaknesses of marriage to Alan.

Good adult educators motivate learners: they inspire, charm and sometimes press individuals into doing more than they expected or thought possible. These are the core skills which Alan brought to NIACE.

Staff and partners were challenged to look a little further and to step outside of conventional frames of reference to take what were usually carefully calculated risks (despite the air of casual brainstorming). Although sometimes one felt bemused, and sometimes infuriated, by the ornate rhetoric and the apparent inability to recognise the impossibility of what was being proposed, the ideas usually worked. It is a style which inspires the loyalty and commitment which was recognised when NIACE became an early organisation to achieve Investor in People (IiP) recognition. But with this has gone a seriously businesslike grasp of detail, of managerial and financial processes. The books balanced, staff were properly treated, the meetings ran, the books and journals continued to flow from the presses. Above all, adult learning was celebrated, with charm, style and conviviality. Although the business, and the work, was hard and long, the experience was of excitement, challenge and celebration. NIACE was fun to work for, and the cause of adult learning as a tool for empowerment and equity, was seriously advanced. This is the gift which Alan brought to NIACE, and which makes those who have worked with him proud to be part of the Institute.

Stephen McNair

Stephen McNair knows Alan Tuckett well. He was Head of UDACE from 1984 until 1992, and Director of Research for NIACE from 1992 to 1998. He is now Professor at the School of Educational Studies at the University of Surrey. This is a personal appreciation of a colleague and friend.

GATHERING STORMS:
HOPES AND REALITIES, 1970–1990

———————

NIACE DURING THE
1970S AND 1980S

Arthur K. Stock

M Y PERIOD AS Director of the Institute extended from July 1971 until April 1988. It began as the last few years of the romantic golden era of traditional education for adults were still offering a warm, optimistic view of the service in the field 'outside', but serviced by and reflected in the style and activities of NIAE (as was its current designation). To some extent, the title of my managerial role when I was appointed, i.e. Secretary to the Institute, epitomised the ethos of a modest servicing body for a cosy world of relatively few professionals and a small army of part-timers and volunteers.

To staff this limited enterprise there were just eight of us: two educational professionals, a skilled publications officer, a librarian and information officer plus administrative and secretarial workers. We were based in the educational servicing enclave of Queen Anne Street in prestigious London W1. Others resident on that pleasant Georgian thoroughfare were the National Foundation for Educational Research (NFER) (soon to leave), the National Council for Audio-Visual Aids in Education and the powerful Association of Education Committees; and most of us were held in financial thrall by the Howard de Walden Estates who owned the whole district. None of those organisations remain there.

I overlapped, for exactly one month, with my dear predecessor, Edward Hutchinson, who 'showed me the ropes'. It was a relatively quiet start to an increasingly hectic and harassing 17 years culminating in a situation in 1988 when NIACE (and its subsidiaries UDACE, REPLAN and ALBSU) employed 80 and 90 staff at any one time.

In 1971 we were 'waiting for Russell', i.e. for the expected Report of the Committee of Enquiry appointed by the Secretary of State for Education and Science under the Chairmanship of Sir Lionel Russell CBE – '…to assess the need for and review the position of non-vocational adult education in England and Wales…'. This document, on which so many hopes rested, did not appear until early 1973. 'Russell' – as it was affectionately called – had many good things to say and to recommend; and, to further the examination and debate, the Institute published a penny broadsheet which sold some 52,000 copies and required 48 sleepless hours from me in order to read the original report and then to summarise it into that four-page form.

This summary-broadsheet was the basic and essential handout at the Institute's main Annual Conference to promote and examine the Report and held at the University College of North Wales (UCNW) in Bangor, and which attracted nearly 500 delegates in April 1973. A little humorous (in retrospect) anecdote attaches to the arrangement of the event, in that the original dates for the Conference agreed between the Institute and UCNW were found by the then Chairman of NIAE Executive to be unacceptable because they clashed with conference dates already arranged (separately) by the Universities' Council of Adult Education (UCAE) and the University of Cambridge to celebrate the centenary of the latter's inception of University Extension in 1873. 'It's obvious,' said this same Chairman to me, 'that if the dates clash, none of the university adult educators will go to Bangor'. I suggested that perhaps Cambridge University might be able to change the UCAE Conference dates; they (and UCAE) were, after all, constituent members of the Institute and stood to gain much from Russell. He looked quite shocked. 'Oh, no,' he said, 'Cambridge could never do *that*'. In the event, the UCNW proved to be more flexible and an alternative later date was found which attracted (I think) the largest number of delegates to any Institute event before or since.

There were further hidden delights in the 1973 Conference emanating from the platform remarks of that same Chairman referred to above, in his reply to the Minister of State sent by the Government of the day to address the delegates. The Minister's speech was a graceful TV-style performance, which said little about the Report and even less about the

Government's response to it. Professor Kelly was very angry, tore up the notes of his originally prepared speech of thanks and, instead, rather castigated the Minister and the present and past Ministries of Education over the years, for their dilettante approach to adult education. In turn this same, normally suave, Minister cornered the Chairman outside the Conference Hall and launched a blistering attack, concluding with, 'A person in your position should be ashamed of such behaviour'.

In these ways are quiet heroes of the Institute made.

The editor of this NIACE 80th Anniversary publication suggested that I might wish to dwell on some of the 'champagne moments' from my 17 years in office. As I have stated elsewhere (*Adult Education*, Vol. 61, No 4) '...such a selection is very difficult to achieve as there were so many issues, though often reiterated, throughout those nearly two decades...'. Moreover, some of the best wines mature slowly and, to continue the analogy, some of the most important events were only recognised as highly rated successes by the Institute some considerable time after the particular 'growing of the wine' and 'bottling the vintage'. Two of these joyful events were: (i) the inception of the government-backed adult literacy programme (and the foundation in 1975 of ALRA under the auspices of the Institute) and (ii) the foundation in 1984, again under Institute auspices, of REPLAN – the agency given the task of addressing the educational needs of unemployed adults and, through regionally based officers (and project money), to stimulate colleges, centres, commercial organisations and voluntary bodies to design programmes accordingly.

Both of these events can only be judged in substantial retrospect. Even in the wilder moments of the *Right to Read* campaign of the mid-1970s (which was centrally organised by the British Association of Settlements, although supported by the collective Institute and several corporate members separately) could we have envisaged the growth of this transformation in 'basic' emphasis in learning through all ages of life as well as the adult years? ALRA, chaired by H D (Billy) Hughes and directed by W A (Bill) Devereux, lasted for three years, working constantly with the BBC and the crucial broadcast element of the campaign as well as with local authority institutions and voluntary bodies throughout England and Wales. ALRA was succeeded by the Adult Literacy Unit

(ALU) as an intermediate construct whilst dialogue with the DES continued (and politics changed). Eventually, it became the Adult Literacy and Basic Skills Unit (ALBSU) and then the fully-fledged Basic Skills Agency (BSA) of the present day, albeit independent of the Institute since 1989.

I well remember being invited by Gerry Fowler, who in late 1974 was Minister of State in the DES, to go up to the House of Commons for an 'important chat' – inevitably in the Bar – to hear of the decision by Government to allocate £1 million (doesn't sound much nowadays, does it?) '...to combat adult illiteracy', and to ask the NIAE to form a suitable agency to undertake the task. The £1 million, by the way, had been carved out of the £3 million or so previously allocated for 'inflation proofing' in respect of the Government's grants to universities. 'It is about time,' said Gerry Fowler, 'that we address the other end of the educational spectrum in post-school provision.'

The other 'champagne moment' was actually a gin and tonic moment, in the bar of Waterloo Station, involving the then Chair of the NIACE Executive Committee, Professor Paul Fordham, and myself. It followed the longest negotiating-with-Ministry-officers session of my whole 17 years at NIACE lasting, as it did, from 2.30 pm until 6.45 pm As well as gaining the resources to found REPLAN (1984–1991) and consequently to achieve a 'regional' presence of capable, innovative and active professional officers, that early evening moment was also a salvage triumph as the Institute very nearly lost the whole of the REPLAN programme, largely through 'mandarin' misinterpretation of debate and discussion in the Institute's Council.

REPLAN and, with a different syntax, UDACE, were pragmatic creations of the Institute (using DES grant money to make them work) devised not only to be workable in the harsh political, social and cultural climate of the 1980s, but also to be better 'change-agents' as compared to what had gone before. We had had the well-meaning but stultified Russell Report in 1973, the creative Venables Report of 1976 (Open University, 1976) and then the huge output of ACACE from 1977 to 1983, culminating in the still-salutary suggestions and constructs of the famous report *Continuing Education: from Policies to Practice* (ACACE, 1982a). Forests of paper (and massive voluntary effort) had been devoted to the production of these Reports – and to numerous similar others by UNESCO, OECD, ICAE, EBAE and the Council of Europe. And yet no holistic change had resulted.

The Institute determined to press for agencies which could 'demonstrate by actual working field projects and schemes – plus careful evaluation' – what might be the way forward in the growing number of sectors in education for adults. This was a sea-change in education development policy, at least in the United Kingdom; and, although both these agencies have long since departed as operating units, their influences are discernible to this day in field practice – perhaps especially in the Further Education colleges. Finally, the prime value of both these 1980s Institute agencies was that, unlike the myriad of 'special' projects – often perceived by politicians and governments as having utilitarian value – they were able to address a multitude of educational targets to meet the needs of those most diverse cohorts of the population, i.e. adults. They were, consequently, closer to 'real life' than the many Ministry (almost every Ministry had one) narrow learning objectives often seen as cheap solutions to achieve political or economic gain.

Thus, after the balmy years of the early to mid-1970s, NIAE/NIACE became more embroiled in the hard graft of field development work in an increasingly cold, sometimes hostile political climate. The Institute's existence was twice directly threatened and was indirectly menaced on even more occasions. My final thoughts are ones of thankfulness that there was, in spite of everything, a healthy – even ebullient – outfit to hand on to the present capable management and direction.

Arthur K Stock

Arthur Stock came to the Institute from Lancashire where he had been County Adviser for Adult Education and having significant experience of Local Education Authorities. He is an enthusiastic sailor and skier upon which he spends much of his spare time. He is an Honorary Life Member of NIACE and a visiting professor to the University of Manchester.

HOW THEY BROUGHT THE GOOD NEWS FROM QUEEN ANNE STREET TO LEICESTER

Henry Arthur Jones

W HEN THE WICKED SQUIRE sent his bailiffs to flourish an expiring lease at the door of Queen Anne Street, demanding an ever-inflating rent, and the fists of the Ministry and the town halls closed ever more tightly on their pelf, gloom overspread the faces of those within.

Arthur spoke to Arthur, Director to Executive Chairman: How *can* we pay? Yet where else in London is there a comparable home that we *can* afford? At all costs the Institute's services to our hard-pressed friends in adult education must be maintained. But why should more of our limited resource be poured into the pocket of a landlord? Then the same answer came into the minds of both the Director (who came from the North-west) and the Chairman (from the East Midlands). Why has it to be London?

By chance an article appeared in a Sunday supplement contrasting property prices in London with those in several provincial cities. A hasty review of the Institute's operations, and especially the membership of its committees, working parties, etc., and where the people came from, suggested that, simply in terms of travelling expenses and time occupied, no hardship would come from a judicious move out of the capital. Birmingham, Manchester, Cambridge, Nottingham, Leicester, Northampton were all looked at. Eventually Leicester was chosen.

Instant murmuring rustled in the undergrowth: didn't the occupant of the Executive Chair have a similar piece of furniture at the University there? Wasn't the deciding factor his convenience in being able to slip so

35 Queen Anne Street

easily from one to the other? In fact it was not so. For one thing it was found that the price of office accommodation was notably cheaper in Leicester than anywhere else. But the final decision came from a piece of commissioned research (sort of). The Chairman's 11-year-old son, a railway enthusiast and incipient Bradshaw, was asked to compile a comparative table of train services from each of the possible centres to and from London, with a comparison of motorway access too. Leicester was quite clearly at the top of these league tables and so negotiation for the lease of 19b De Montfort Street began forthwith.

So it was that the emblematic address of NIACE passed from Queen Anne, remembered for little but her legs in every antiques shop, to Simon De Montfort, champion against the centralising authority of the monarchy. *Floreat exemplum.*

Henry Arthur Jones

(Henry) Arthur Jones is Emeritus Professor at the University of Leicester. He was the Institute's Executive Chairman when the move from London to Leicester took place. An early supporter and member of the Institute – he was present at the 'birth' of NIACE in 1949, and is now an Honorary Life Member of NIACE.

A FRIENDLY LODGER (ACACE) FROM
1977–1983

Howard Gilbert

T HIS YEAR'S CELEBRATION of NIACE's 80th birthday must include a commentary upon the quaintly described NIACE's 'children', (NIACE, 1999). UDACE and REPLAN (not an acronym) are the subject of studies elsewhere in this publication. This review seeks to focus ACACE as a major contributor to the quiet revolution now well advanced in creating a national, unified system of post-16 further and adult education and training.

The 'offspring' attribution is poetic licence; the Council was not even a stepchild! Members were appointed in a personal capacity, and ACACE reported directly to the Secretary of State for Education and Science. In 1977 this was Shirley Williams; her successor, Mark Carlisle, renewed the mandate in 1980, and the final report was sent to Sir Keith Joseph in 1983.

The notion of 'child status' derives from two circumstances. First, four of the members (Peter Clyne, Howard Gilbert, H.D. (Billy) Hughes, and Professor Henry Arthur Jones) served also on the Institute's Council. Second, NIAE had spare office space in its old headquarters, and the Department accepted the offer. The outcome of this bargain was announced in *Adult Education* (Vol.50 No.4):

> *The Council's address, for all communications, is 19b De Montfort Street, Leicester, LE1 7GE.*

Derek Legge in his history *The Education of Adults in Britain* (1982) says that the sharing of office accommodation seems to have helped both by enabling close relationships and the joint use of information resources available at the Institute. The situation was a constructive one, reinforced in part by the fact that the NIAE Director, Arthur K Stock, was also an Assessor – one of five – to the Council. Undoubtedly these connections are the origin of the subsequent assumption of 'filial' status.

The Advisory Council's remit was to advise generally upon the national provision of education for adults; to promote co-operation between providers; to review current practice, organisation and priorities,

> *with the view to the most effective use of available resources…and to promote the development of future policies for 'education as a process continuing throughout life.'*

The Russell Committee (1973) had recommended a national development council; the Secretary of State at the time (Margaret Thatcher) did not respond, despite the great hopes which this recommendation aroused amongst field workers and local authorities alike. When the Advisory Council was appointed four years later expectations were enormous.

The possibility of a brighter prospect increased with the appointment of Dr. Richard Hoggart as Chairman; a distinguished scholar, renowned for his seminal text *The Uses of Literacy*, and for his writing about, and contributions to, adult education teacher training. In his earlier career he was Assistant Director General of UNESCO, and before that an Extra-Mural Tutor at the University of Hull. He was known to be a strong Europhile, and was shortly to become Warden of Goldsmiths College in the University of London. His other attributes included powerful advocacy of the Arts. From the Institute's position this appointment also gave some encouragement. NIAE was developing the European and international legacy of its previous chief officer, Edward Hutchinson. Throughout the 'field' the prospects were felt to be encouraging.

Richard Hoggart brought to the Council and shared a great breadth of knowledge and understanding of the issues of the time: both the need for a larger appreciation of the term 'continuing education', and a sharp awareness of the pressures being experienced by liberal adult non-vocational education. Drawing upon this reservoir of philosophy, good practice and wide understanding, he was able to meld a disparate group of people, officially non-representative of interests, but each having concerns related to them, into a constructive, committed, voluntary and capable team.

The ACACE members belonged to a broad spectrum of English and Welsh professional people: from manufacturing industry, the Confederation of British Industry (CBI), the Trade Union Congress (TUC) and local government; from the media (television and radio), the arts and libraries, and the adult student body whose representative came from the ECA. They included elected councillors, people from voluntary agencies and women's organisations, together with those from the ethnic minorities. Finally the 'mix' of these 22 members contained practitioners from higher and further education and training, and liberal adult, non-vocational education reflecting, respectively, the university and local authority traditions.

The Council's annual budget was £50,000 in its first year. This was to provide a secretariat, research associates if needed, all operating expenses, consultations, visits, travel and all other items necessary to a body engaged in public enquiries. Additionally, since ACACE publications were distributed mainly free of charge, the cost of this was met from the budget. The Council faced situations calling for immediate representation and informed reporting; there were longer-term issues passed over from the 1973 Russell Report, and the responses that it had invoked. In the 'field' much uncertainty about the future obtained: public purse strings were being tightened.

John Taylor, the intelligent, dedicated, hard-working and seemingly tireless Secretary of the Council for most of its six-year term, brought to his work the constructive, practical experience of his tenure with the Scottish Institute of Adult Education. He pinpointed the Council's initial dilemmas, and some of its action, in an article for *Adult Education* (Vol. 51 No.4).

Our first year has been absorbed in identifying all the many issues which members want to tackle and facing up to the hard job of putting these issues in some order of priority. Some…of pressing importance have already received attention and have been the subject of formal statements to the Secretary of State. In this way we have sought to give prominence to the recent inequitable cuts in adult education financial provision, to the dangers of adults passing out of the sphere of local authority education committees into a world of leisure and recreation, and to the real difficulties facing the invaluable work of voluntary bodies because of the current economic stringencies.

…the Council's arrival on the scene could probably not have been at an economically less auspicious moment at any time in the past twenty-five years. So there was the immediate task of trying to hold the line. At the same time in the other direction lay the broadening horizon of interest in making greater sense of the wholeness of post-school education, which can stem from making a reality out of the present vaguely designed idea of continuing education. And somewhere between, lay all the problems being encountered now in planning for early changes and improvements in the education of adults.

What did the council achieve?

I recall that, in this first year of analysis and ordering, responding the while to urgent issues, we were able to meet quarterly in full session with small working groups functioning between as the member's professional commitments allowed. The tensions of these time and space problems were, however, present throughout much of the six-year term. Undoubtedly they inspired the title of a final paper – written by Professor Naomi Sargant (McIntosh) – listing the Council's achievements: *In the Corners of our Time*[1]. This was not scratching around, as one interpretation of that phrase might suggest, but committed, involved, thorough-going work in the best tradition of voluntary service in the community.

---

1 '*In The Corners of Our Time*' is the title of an analysis listing the reports, public statements, occasional and discussion papers, produced by the council during its six-year term. It was annexed to, and published separately from, the personal statement of the Chairman in October 1983. It documents, in a formal fashion, the scale of the Council's work, given that all its members, and many of those who participated in its working or consultative groups, were volunteers, mostly engaged in full-time employment.

The analysis and writing is that of Professor Naomi Sergeant, now Visiting Professor to the Open University, and Honorary Senior Research Fellow of NIACE.

Almost beyond the call of duty some members accepted extra 'watching briefs' to cover limited areas of adult education interest which had a potential close link with the continuing work of both the immediate and the longer term study committees: respectively 'A' and 'B'. These briefs were: adult basic education, adult education and the churches, education and training for young adults, pre- and post-retirement education, public libraries and adult education, and issues relating to women's opportunities for education and training.

The ACACE papers are deposited at the Public Record Office; copies of its minutes, related transactions and publications are also in the NIACE Archive. There were 36 reports, public statements of concern, reports to the Secretary of State on the Council's directly commissioned work, occasional papers, research findings including two very large programmes that directly influenced the Council's major report: *Continuing Education: from Policies to Practice* (1982). Both NIACE's legitimate 'children' owe their existence to the Council's work: REPLAN, a programme of education to assist the unemployed, and UDACE, which was born in 1984, after ACACE's work had ended. In addition, ALU had its role extended and its title changed to ALBSU – later to become the BSA, a free-standing 'adult' independent from NIACE. These were considerable achievements; they represented also the 'broadening horizon of interest' to which John Taylor referred in his notes about the Council's first year.

Roger Fieldhouse, the contemporary historian of modern British adult education, provides an assessment of the ACACE work, 14 years on from its conclusion:

> *Despite its modest resources it managed to make some significant contributions to the direction of adult continuing education… it saw itself as an authoritative voice for the education of adults which could make itself heard at the highest level of policy making.*
>
> *The Council's most significant Report was 'Continuing Education: From Policies to Practice'.*

This report was described in the Education Press as one of the most important adult education publications since Russell and Alexander. It was the work of Committee 'B' convened by Professor Naomi Sargant (McIntosh). She largely carried out the task of writing the final document under great pressure, supported by the Secretary to the Council, John Taylor.

The Report was backed by a detailed statistical survey and analysis written by the convenor and prepared, to be published later as *Adults: Their educational experience and needs* (ACACE, 1982b). A further source of information and knowledge from which *Policies to Practice* (as the field called it) drew, was the extensive research and mapping project of the education services and facilities for adults, in the North-West of England. This was the work of a group at Lancaster University, led by Keith Percy and convened by ACACE member, Richard Smethurst. Both research projects were part of a DES-funded major enquiry into the education of adults. Hailed as a 'milestone' at a time when the education of adults seemed to be moving further down the scale of priorities, the report can be regarded – and should so be – as the fertile soil, carefully sown, in which – with some extra compost, tilling and further preparation – the recent newly grafted and cultivated system for the education and training of adults is starting to take root. There are numerous 'cultivars' that contribute to the metaphor: two recent reports *Learning in the 21st Century* (NAGCELL, 1997), *Learning Works* (Kennedy/FEFC, 1997), and the FEFC's 26 pilot studies on *Widening Participation* are of immediate relevance. Others include both the responses to these Reports, and – for example – *Accountability in Further Education* (DfEE, 1998), published by the DfEE, plus the recent legislation establishing the national and sub-regional Learning and Skills Councils. Each of these draws, wittingly or not, upon the garden of thoughts, ideas, practices and proposals produced in ACACE's major report, outlining a possible system of continuing education.

The Council's other work was equally extensive and detailed. Fieldhouse notes the interest it had in credit transfer systems, the application of new technology, open and distance learning, access to higher education, independent study, grants to part-time students, and an education entitlement for adults. Papers and short publications were produced on adult education and the black communities, basic science and basic mathematics, local learning centres, and a review of teacher training needs together with a study of qualifications awarded by voluntary specialist organisations that contribute to leisure-time skills, sports and physical fitness.

A prime concern was mature entry to university courses. The Chairman wrote a brief paper arguing the case for greater diversity following post-war expansion. This among the very first commentaries to be published by the Council. Two reports reviewed political education, the second of which looked at West Germany. (The Committee was convened by H.D. (Billy) Hughes and directly clerked by the Secretary who consulted the four main political parties: Conservative, Labour, Liberal and Social Democrat.) The outcome was a view that more classes were needed in the Politics of Democracy; the Council so advised. However, a Minister of the Crown thought this provision would be a form of 'red indoctrination'! A comprehensive review of Information, Counselling and Guidance Services was carried out and proposals made for their development. Studies in the arts, local radio, and volunteers in adult education make up the balance. In very many ways the Council's work foreshadowed future developments at the end of the century.

About three months before the Council's mandate became due for renewal, members were dismayed to learn that its major report was unlikely to find favour with the Secretary of State, Sir Keith Joseph, and hence the Government. There was also, as Fieldhouse records, a view among professionals in the liberal adult education that the report placed that particular element of continuing education at risk. As is apparent, almost 20 years later, the report 'got it largely right' and history may well document as serious error Sir Keith Joseph's rejection. However, there still remains the doubt among professionals, to which Roger Fieldhouse gave expression.

The anguish of the Chairman, shared by all Council members, was expressed in his personal statement, sent to the Secretary of State, in October 1983, at the end of the Council's term of appointment. He wrote:

> It is a sad paradox that ACACE has spent most of its six-year life, in which it has proved beyond doubt the need for great increases in continuing education support by a national Development Body, during the term of a government which has proved unwilling to be so persuaded.

It is not too much to assert that the Eighties should see the full start of a process, which will eventually dissolve the 'end-on' view of education in favour of a view of education as a process continuously available and, by very many people used, for varied purposes throughout life.

In his final paragraph Richard Hoggart looks forward to a prospect of future achievement. In words that are almost prescient he concludes the Statement:

We have a national habit of arguing against a plainly good thing until the last minute then, once we have grasped the case, of doing a volte-face and going further, faster, than anyone would have predicted. This should be such a moment.

The moment was not ... but now – in the 80th year of NIACE and its predecessors – 'is'. The 'process continuously available, and by very many people used, for varied purposes throughout life' is beginning to be put in place. Alan Tuckett, in a commentary in *Adults Learning* during 2000, notes of the Bill, now an Act, that the 'devil is in the detail'. I take that to mean that the basis of a continuing education system for adults is there to be found and developed. Someone, of a different frame of mind,

The final meeting of ACACE – Richard Hoggart in the chair

remarked in a recent meeting "much is up for grabs". Given the speed and pace of change since 1998, a rationale for that observation can easily be found. The opportunity to achieve a comprehensive structure is there, provided also – and for this reason the Advisory Council's membership included an adult student – the present Secretary of State's vision of learner involvement becomes a corner stone of the building. In celebrating NIACE we celebrate ACACE too.

Dr. Richard Hoggart, Peter Clyne, Professor Naomi Sargant (McIntosh), and Professor Henry Arthur Jones are all Honorary Life Members of NIACE. Richard Smethurst is Provost of Worcester College, Oxford and President of NIACE.

Professor Naomi Sargant is visiting Professor to the Open University and Honorary Senior Research Fellow of NIACE.

Howard Gilbert

Howard Gilbert was a member of ACACE from 1977 to 1983. He convened the committees which reviewed part-time tutor training; that researched and reported upon volunteers in adult education; and that produced the Council's report on local learning centres. He was a member also of Committee 'B' convened by Naomi Sargant, which produced the report 'Continuing Education: From Policies to Practice'.

WISE PRESIDENTIAL GUIDANCE IN A TIME OF TURBULENCE: 1988-1994

Sir Roy Harding

L ADY PLOWDEN, my predecessor as President, wrote to me early in 1988, and I met her for lunch in London, where she told me that NIACE had just appointed Alan Tuckett, whom I knew of but didn't know, and after a suggested lunch with Alan and Peter Clyne, the then Chairman of the Executive Committee, and some private enquiries, including to the Honorary Treasurer, Ken Brooksbank, ex-Chief Education Officer for Birmingham, whom I knew well, I agreed to be President. Alan struck me as an able and realistic visionary and I was very impressed with his views about the way ahead. There was a great deal to do and many relationships to be built.

Unfortunately many of my clearest memories of my period with NIACE was of the continuing loss of units which it helped to set up – a process which had gone on for many years. The first to go in my period was ALBSU, which had had a very close association with NIACE. The Secretary of State announced in the middle of 1990 that ALBSU was to have corporate and charitable status as an independent body. Various reasons were given for this, but I always thought it was partly because Peter Davis, now Chairman of Sainsbury's, had been asked to be Chairman of ALBSU without – so he told me, when I went to see him to ask whether he would be willing to continue the practice of coming to NIACE Executive meetings – being told anything about the relationship with NIACE. I was not surprised; he said that he wouldn't have time to attend these meetings. I suppose, too, that he had thought there would be for ALBSU the direct link with the then DES and may have been unhappy that there might be some intermediate group considering ALBSU's activities. Clearly Alan and Alan Wells (ALBSU's Director) did a great deal of work, work leading to the new constitution and functions for ALBSU and the consequent actions by NIACE including enabling the needed transfer of assets, though I remember a number of meetings with the then Under-Secretary at the DES and I think I remarked on the goodwill of the many members and staff of NIACE in spite of their disquiet at the March 1991 split.

I often wondered whether the action of splitting ALBSU from NIACE didn't partly cause the outcome of the review of UDACE in 1991, namely an acknowledgement of NIACE's great help in setting up and managing it since 1984 but deciding that, with all the changes resulting from the White Paper Education and Training in the 21st Century and the setting up of the FEFC it would be better that the research and development activities should be managed by the body responsible for curriculum developments, the FEU. Consequently came the letter to me in June 1991 from Tim Eggar, then Minister of State, saying this is what the Secretary of State had decided. I do not remember what Dick Smethurst, then UDACE Chairman, now NIACE President, thought of this, but those of us in NIACE didn't like it at all, nor do I think did the small group who worked in UDACE.

During the same period the Government decided not to continue with the REPLAN programme after seven years of success. When Alan Tuckett, Tony Uden (who headed REPLAN) and I went to see Tim Eggar at the end of 1990 and made suggestions to him about alternatives it seemed to us that, unfortunately, he was not open to suggestions – indeed it looked as if he had somehow been briefed or at least thought that we had come perhaps as a formality to object to any idea of change. So, in October 1991, REPLAN vanished from NIACE control, though fortunately Tony was found an active post within NIACE.

Perhaps I'm unkind to Tim Eggar and really he was looking for ways to justify continuing the annual grant from DES to NIACE. Throughout my time as President there were annual pilgrimages to the representatives of the Local Authority Associations to request an annual grant from them, with much paper from Alan to them and to the DES, seeking to justify our requests. (Normally the grants from the DES and the Local Authorities were at the same level.) It seemed in those early days hard work to achieve a continuation of a similar grant and virtually impossible to achieve any much needed increase. It was a great relief late in 1991 to have a letter from Tim Eggar saying that DES would continue their annual grant at the same level, though they wished to be more specific about the ways in which the grant should be spent. This approach probably arose because of the review of NIACE by the Local Authority Associations, which, as was to be expected, particularly after some good spadework by Alan, was generally supportive and complementary.

Perhaps Alan had established himself by this time, but I felt that after this point NIACE received a more sympathetic ear not only from the DES, where Tim Boswell had taken over as the Minister responsible for adult education, but also from the Local Authority Associations. We lost the advantage of an adult education inside-voice at the DES, when the Further Education Inspectorate was abolished in 1993 and, in spite of very good arguments, largely developed by Alan, we only slowly managed to persuade the DES and LEAs to provide some extra resources, for example to help the long-delayed move into better premises, helped by the knowledge that Alan was contriving to find resources from other places for other projects.

Compared with many other things, the constitutional changes for NIACE must have seemed to many unimportant. Nevertheless the development to a registered company limited by guarantee and as a registered charity were important for those with whom we sought to deal. A great deal of the credit for this work needs to go to Shiela Carlton, who joined NIACE soon after I became President. Her work in helping to set up a good structure of committees and sub-committees to assist all kinds of adult education participants to be involved or at least recognise their views were represented and taken seriously was excellent. There were times when Alan's considerable powers of persuasion had to be used to ensure acceptance, but I do believe that the combination of Alan as Director and Shiela as Secretary was a very good one and I suspect that without her Alan would not have had the time to develop NIACE and its external relationships so successfully.

Others will be able to write with much more knowledge than I of the development of a first-class and rapidly expanding publications section, highlighted by *Adults Learning*, of the development of a very good research element of NIACE, both by means of externally funded work and by work from the Association's own staff (a particular area in which Alan was an excellent guiding light) and the development of a sound financial basis.

Behind it all was Alan's leadership and desire to improve the knowledge and conception of adult education everywhere and to increase numbers and improve the quality of adult learning in every part of the community. This ranged from developing the All-Party Parliamentary Group for Adult Education, briefing ministers – and Opposition – and a variety of national bodies, supporting the expansion and recognition of NIACE Cymru, extending the programme of conferences from the annual weekend at a University and autumn day conference at the Glaziers' Hall, setting up and developing the annual Adult Learners' Week and in this as in so many other areas, promoting international activities and understanding… The list could extend greatly. But I remember most his concern, and that of his staff, always to seek ways of persuading others, especially those disadvantaged in any way, that, in the words of the later Helena Kennedy report *Learning Works* (Kennedy, 1997).

I believed I saw him developing NIACE into an excellent powerhouse for adult education.

Sir Roy Harding

Sir Roy Harding became President of NIACE in 1988, when there was much uncertainty about the future for the education of adults, and soon after Alan Tuckett's appointment as Director, in succession to Arthur Stock.

He had retired at the end of a distinguished career as Chief Education Officer for Buckinghamshire – an LEA with a sensitive and committed community education service in a rapidly changing society situated in small towns, centres of industry, a new city development, and rural villages with significant agricultural and commuter populations.

At this critical time, Sir Roy brought to NIACE the experience, wisdom and constructive advice that enabled the Institute and its Director to renew energies and refocus services to meet successfully the challenge of the 1990s. This letter is his personal testament and response to the NIACE 80th Anniversary.

*Sir Roy Harding presenting an award to
Jeannie Sutcliffe*

SIR WINSTON CHURCHILL (1953)
ON ADULT EDUCATION

T HERE IS PERHAPS no branch of our vast educational system which should more attract within its particular sphere than adult education. How many must there be in Britain, after the disturbance of two destructive wars, who thirst in later life to learn about the humanities, the history of their country, the philosophies of the human race, and the arts and letters which sustain and are borne forward by the ever-conquering English language?

This ranks in my opinion far above science and technical instruction which are well sustained and not without their rewards in our present system. The mental and moral outlook of free men studying the past with free minds in order to discern the future demands the highest measures, which our hard-pressed finances can sustain. I have no doubt myself that a man or woman earnestly seeking in grown-up life to be guided to wide and suggestive knowledge in its largest and most uplifted sphere will make the best of all the pupils in this age of clatter and buzz, of gape and gloat. The appetite of adults to be shown the foundations and processes of thought will never be denied by a British administration cherishing the continuity of our island life.

But there are no reasons for not looking through the accounts and making sure that all we can give is turned to real advantage.

Accompanying his letter, Sir Roy Harding sent a copy of Sir Winston Churchill's 1953 commentary on the need for adult education.

Almost 47 years on, it still has a number of very contemporary messages to offer. I suspect that most of us, today, would demur at the opening words of the second paragraph, and we might wonder also at the distance of time between such a statement of necessity, and the recent commencement of the Parliamentary process to secure its achievement.

However, as a number of contributors to this publication have emphasised, and in the words of one of them: 'The main reason for the failure in the early post-war years to secure the anticipated significant expansion in adult education lay of course, in the shortage of available public funding'. Nevertheless Sir Winston's statement has an honourable place in this celebration of the NIACE 80th Anniversary.

Editor

REPLAN AND UDACE …
THE 'BARONIES'

REPLAN – AN EDUCATION PROGRAMME
FOR THE ADULT UNEMPLOYED

Tony Uden

W HEN ALAN TUCKETT was appointed Director of NIACE in 1988, George Low, writing in *Education*, compared him to a king whose newly-acquired throne was beset by over-mighty barons. That one of these 'baronies' was REPLAN was a back-handed compliment to those who had steered the Programme from small and shaky beginnings to a position where it commanded a larger budget and staff than the core of NIACE itself.

George also failed to appreciate how the leadership provided by Paul Fordham (Chair) and Arthur Stock (Director), in those early years when Paul combined the position of NIACE Executive Chair with that of REPLAN, had ensured that the Programme not only fulfilled the objectives of its Government founders and progenitors, but also strengthened its adoptive parent, allowing NIACE to play some of the roles it had aspired to over many years.

REPLAN had its origins in the Government's belated and pusillanimous response to the final report of ACACE. In its origins and its subsequent development it is perhaps a text book example of the tensions within the adult education 'movement'. While Alan had been among the most vocal opponents of NIACE's acceptance of the 'chalice', (either because it was poisoned or not full enough and probably a combination of both) and John Field was to say that REPLAN 'reeked of rank political opportunism', others saw it as an opportunity to show what adult educators could achieve given half a chance. (All involved were aware that it was only half a chance.)

There had been other national initiatives to target particular groups, most notably the ALBSU, at the time still an agency of NIACE. However, the tradition of a locally administered and, to a large extent, locally determined education service was still strong in those pre-1992 days. The Institute had to be sensitive to the view of many providers – including local authorities who were an influential body among its members – that they already knew how to do the job and merely needed to be given the resources and left to get on with it.

Nevertheless, the processes of development, co-ordination, curriculum leadership, advocacy, staff development and sheer promotion embarked upon in 1984 have had a profound effect on the way adult learning is generally perceived; the effects of REPLAN can be felt to this day.

With a tiny budget of £100,000 from the DES, supplemented with £70,000 from the Welsh Office and the Manpower Services Commission (MSC), the Institute's REPLAN was launched. At the beginning larger sums than this were given to the Further Education Unit (FEU) and the Open University (OU) but it is worth noting that when the Programme closed after seven exciting and sometimes turbulent years, NIACE's budget for REPLAN, of about £1,250,000 made it by far the senior partner.

REPLAN, with its remit to *promote education and training for unemployed adults*, was open to sniping from both sides of the political divide. Two remarkable civil servants, Noel Thompson and Gordon Etheridge, had the job of justifying the ways of REPLAN to those members of the Thatcher Administration who accused us of fostering a culture of benefit dependency. From the other side the same people who opposed 'Government interference' were also loud in their criticism of the meagre budget, while the Naïve Tendency on the left was further outraged by the acceptance of MSC money since they were able to distinguish 'clean' Government money – of the kind which flowed to university departments – from the tainted lucre of the MSC. Criticism of the clumsy, narrow and often downright insulting nature of some of the Government's training programmes was sometimes allowed to spill over into criticism of any educational effect which could be construed as preparing adults for work, including those parts of REPLAN that did this. These were heady days indeed.

NIACE's initial role in REPLAN was to select and administer a series of projects and, while these remained an important testing ground for new ideas, their early prominence dogged the future by reinforcing the notion that REPLAN was to pay for the provision of education for three million unemployed, with £170,000! This incensed first those projects sponsors whose good ideas could not be funded and then those whose successful experimental work was not funded on a continuing basis.

As the DES's ideas for the programme unfolded (influenced increasingly by NIACE – as mutual trust developed), the whole thing became more coherent, but the early decision to divide the management between three partners was never resolved even when NIACE became so pre-eminently the senior partner.

Funds were made available for Regional Field Officers to be managed by NIACE – perhaps the best news that the Institute had had for many years – and later these were supported by administrative as well as secretarial staff. A real presence was now possible across the counties of England and Wales. Education Support Grants (ESGs) were made available to LEAs for their work with the unemployed. The funds were used mainly to appoint local REPLAN workers. But here also clarity on their relationship to the Field Officers was never fully achieved; they proved happy to be co-ordinated by them on a regional basis and most looked to the NIACE Field Officer for professional support if not direction. The small budgets devolved to the Field Officers also helped to give them influence in their regions if they were able to take it – and most of them were.

When a substantial budget for staff development was also made available, drawing an even wider circle of practitioners into the REPLAN orbit, it was possible to establish extensive networks across local authorities and their adult services and colleges. The staff development programme was co-ordinated nationally, delivered regionally and the whole informed by the development of training resources for teachers meeting, for the first time, the issues raised by unemployed adult students.

One of the first project publications from FEU, *Adult Unemployment and the Curriculum*, (FEU/REPLAN, 1985) provided a firm base for taking the work forward (though there was much heart-searching before a formula could be found by which to include political education under another name). The whole was underpinned by national and regional conferences and publications.

By the second year of the programme two principles had become clear; these were to guide the work for the remainder of its life. Firstly that the Programme was about 'change':

> ... *the programme will stand or fall by the measure of its success in bringing about change throughout the adult continuing education system which makes that system more able and more willing to serve the needs of adult unemployed students.'*
>
> (Uden in Adult Education VOL. 60, 1)

Secondly, and less loudly trumpeted, REPLAN was promoting ideas and ways of working which were relevant to the much wider constituency of adult working class students. Within that, the unemployed, those with learning difficulties, black people and those suffering the double discrimination of being poor and female. The Programme was addressing the NIACE agenda and one, which the Institute shared with the majority of providers, of adult continuing education.

In addition to their regional responsibilities the field officers took on national roles: for the staff development, for rural areas, for women, for the black and minority ethnic unemployed. For the few black staff engaged in the work, a small bursary fund was set up to facilitate their attendance at REPLAN events. Some of these had their own national advisory groups like the *Forum for the Advancement of Education and Training for the Black Unemployed* (FAETBU).

It has been argued the REPLAN was swimming with the demographic tide in persuading institutions, especially colleges, to take in more adult students. It was even said that REPLAN did more for its staff than its clients. Not so: I am absolutely convinced that the speed, volume and culture of the process of change, which is still taking place in post-school education, was deeply affected by the Programme.

It is true also that many senior colleagues in adult and further education today cut their radical teeth on the REPLAN Programme as ESG workers, field officers or trainers. This has surely been a beneficial influence for millions of adults now learning in mainstream institutions. The Kennedy Report was heavily influenced by people whose ideas had been developed through the REPLAN experience. Among other things it resolved the tension between targeting curriculum areas like basic skills and targeting communities like poor or the unemployed, by pointing out that those in need of the one usually resided in the other.

After a remarkable run of convinced or persuadable Conservative junior Ministers at the DES, in 1991 REPLAN came up against a politician of a different stripe, was condemned unheard, and closed. The proposal developed by the REPLAN committee for a new programme: *People, Learning and Jobs* – which would have begun to bridge the artificial divide between those actually unemployed and the much larger number of people whose lives, in all aspects, not just employment, are diminished by lack of educational opportunity – was barely discussed outside NIACE circles. Our fundamental concern was galloping structural unemployment, the existence of which the Government did not accept. For us the end was nigh.

I am convinced that REPLAN is an episode in its history of which the Institute can be proud. The influence it has had is considerable, almost wholly beneficial and is still being felt. It enabled NIACE to have regional arms, national specialist expertise, funding to back innovation and experiment, money to oil the wheels and support the smallest voluntary efforts, and a programme of staff development for those wanting to improve their skills in working with neglected communities which had been part of its aspirations for many years.

Since 1997 some of these possibilities have again proved practicable: an expanded cadre of specialist Development Officers, the Adult and Community Learning Fund (ACLF) and other funding initiatives together with the first steps in securing staff development programmes and a regional presence.

Once Alan Tuckett, the new Director in 1988, understood the radical orientation which REPLAN had taken and the possibilities for expanded activity for NIACE it had opened up in an otherwise unfriendly environment, he became wholly supportive of its efforts. Under his leadership NIACE's political clout has grown hugely and the lessons of REPLAN –

modified to suit the times but still there in their essentials – remain the ones that NIACE and its members press upon Governments and providers.

Tony Uden

Tony Uden managed the REPLAN project from its inception in 1984 until its demise in 1991 when the Minister of State decided not to renew the scheme despite NIACE proposals for its development. Tony continued with NIACE as an Associate Director, and is now a part-time senior research fellow with the Institute.

UDACE – UNIT FOR THE DEVELOPMENT OF
ADULT CONTINUING EDUCATION

Stephen McNair

I N 1983 ACACE concluded its existence, publishing its ambitious proposals for action after six years of deliberation. As its outgoing Chairman, Richard Hoggart, observed, 'Government does not need more
advice, now we need some action'. Government's response, after some
time for thought, was not to create a large free-standing national agency,
but to invite NIACE to house a development unit, initially with an annual
development budget of £50,000 pa, rather than the £6m proposed by
ACACE.

The leaders of ACACE were insulted, both by the scale of the money,
and the decision to link the Unit to NIACE. The Institute had no recent
track record of major developmental activity, and was, at the time, perceived as interested in a relatively small corner of the post-school learning
world. ACACE members, and many within NIACE, advised rejecting the
proposal, but the Institute, urged by civil servants who suggested that this
was both the best deal on offer, and the thin end of a potentially large
wedge, took a more pragmatic view, and in June 1984 UDACE was born.

From the beginning UDACE was seen as both a part of, and independent of, NIACE. Unlike previous initiatives which had grown organi-
cally from within the Institute, UDACE had a separate budget and a
Steering Committee appointed by the DES and not accountable to the
NIACE Committee structure. Its staff (initially Stephen McNair as Head
of Unit, and Sandra Silver as Administrator) were NIACE employees, and
its accounts were handled through NIACE, but the Committee could, and
did, take its own position on priorities and strategies. The Department

appointed Don Grattan to Chair the Unit, and he used the skills refined by a long career in Educational Broadcasting at the BBC to steer the delicate politics of the relationships with NIACE and DES through the Unit's eight years of life.

UDACE focused on a small number of key topics, working in a concentrated way on about three at any one time, and tackling each over two to three years (with the exception of educational guidance, which never left the agenda). The initial topics were proposed by the DES (guidance, older learners, voluntary/ statutory partnerships) but later ones emerged from debates within the Steering Committee. Topics were kept on the live agenda for two or three years, and then replaced with new ones The Unit adopted a collaborative approach, recognising that UDACE and NIACE staff and members could not themselves be expert on all the issues. So for each topic a broad-based Development Group was created, with membership crossing the traditional sectoral and institutional boundaries. Each Group was chaired by a member of the UDACE Steering Committee, and usually one or two full-time staff were recruited to lead the work. Each group surveyed its field, identified priorities, mounted project work, and produced critical studies and recommendations. By this means, over the eight-year life of the Unit, over 500 practitioners from all sectors and parts of the United Kingdom were actively involved in the work, which generated over 60 reports.

Some people expected UDACE to concentrate exclusively on the developmental areas of NIACE's traditional LEA and WEA/University adult education territory, but the Steering Committee never accepted this boundary. The Unit increasingly sought to tackle issues which extended across the full range of adult learning, diversifying its funding to support this, undertaking 13 major externally-funded projects in addition to the core DES-funded activity.

Its first, and longest lasting, development topic demonstrates why this was. A national structure for educational guidance would need to touch on formal, informal and non-formal providers of learning opportunities in public, private and voluntary sectors, and this was reinforced by the first large scale national study of advice and guidance needs, led by Judy Alloway and commissioned from UDACE by the Employment

Department. It also became clear that no existing agency had a sufficiently broad remit to carry development forward. So, after a national consultative exercise, in 1986 UDACE published its major proposals in *The Challenge of Change*, recommending the creation of a national agency. The Employment Department persuaded the DES to share the cost of the National Educational Guidance Initiative (NEGI), as a unit within UDACE. The Unit and NEGI, led by Vivienne Rivis, laid the foundations for what became a major priority for public education policy in the 1990s, doing the groundwork for the creation of the three key elements of guidance since 1997 – cross-sectoral standards for staff and for services, and the National Guidance Council.

Access to education was a second major theme of the Unit's work. Again cross-sectoral working was a feature, with particular emphasis on the emerging themes of accreditation. The Unit was involved in the creation of the national framework for the recognition of access courses, and David Browning and Caroline Mager were recruited to carry out a major project to establish and consolidate the then fragile national network of Open Colleges. Toni Fazaeli was recruited to undertake and disseminate a series of case studies of good practice as *Innovation in Access* (UDACE, 1991). The studies sought to highlight exciting practice and common themes across a range of contexts stretching from Universities and LEAs to a Housing Association and a Trades Union.

Probably the most controversial project which UDACE undertook sprang from the Access area. In 1987, a senior civil servant visited Alverno College in Milwaukee. There he saw in use higher education entry selection tools, developed from commercial personnel interviewing techniques, which he thought might speed up the process of entry to higher education for non-traditional learners. UDACE was sceptical but after some persuasion agreed reluctantly to undertake an evaluation, and Sue Otter joined the Unit to lead the Student Potential Project. The combination of commercial selection tools and a radical adult education clientele proved philosophically and politically explosive and the project saw two years of fierce debate. Ultimately the tools proved effective at identifying key personal qualities, but far too expensive to meet the Government's need for quick and cheap alternatives to access courses. However, the question which it raised, of what constitutes success in higher education (against which to measure entry selection procedures), took on a new life. The result was the national project on *Learning Outcomes in Higher Education*, which began the continuing quest to make higher education more accessible by making its processes and outcomes transparent to all its stakeholders. Ten years after the demise of UDACE, these ideas form a core element of the national quality assurance framework for higher education.

Other themes also featured. Bob Powell led a body of work based around the two major parliamentary Bills of 1988 and 1992, analysing the drafts, briefing the NIACE political lobbying process and advising the field on implications. The possibility that LEAs might be required to provide formal definitions of 'adequate provision of adult education' led many Officers to undertake reviews and planning exercises not before considered, and as with many areas of the Unit's work, making practitioners ask themselves to examine their practice and reflect on it with others from very different backgrounds led to real changes in some places.

Over 500 people were involved directly in UDACE's work, and many have gone on to play leading roles on the national or local scene. The 15 full-time development staff who worked at some stage for the Unit included Roger Harrison on older learners, Carole Barnes on educational guidance and Kathryn Ecclestone on assessment. The members of the Steering Committee, themselves drawn from a very wide field, also played a key role. The chairs of the development and project groups included Jonathan Brown from the OU; Barbara Saunders of the WI; Judith Summers from Macclesfield College; three Vice-Chancellors (Peter Toyne, Clive Booth and Ray Cowell); two LEA officers (David Hibbert from Surrey and Eddie Burch from Kent), Jeanne Bisgood who had served on ACACE, Eileen Aird from Hillcroft College; and two Chief Education Officers (Alan Culley from Knowsley and Peter Boulter from Cumbria).

In 1992, Ministers decided that UDACE had extended its brief beyond comfortable limits, and undertook a tidying-up exercise, merging the Unit with the FEU, and relocating a small core of staff to London. The attempt to combine the deliberately broad agenda of UDACE with the much more sharply-focused FE one of FEU proved difficult, but before the new structure had settled down, a new move was made to merge FEU with the FE Staff College. The resulting agency, with a strong focus on the FE sector emerged, in 1993, as the Further Education Development Agency (FEDA), transforming itself again in 2001 into the Learning and Skills Development Agency (LSDA).

UDACE was a child of its time. At a point when adult learning was emerging from the political wilderness, and about to invade unsuspecting sectors of education, the Unit laid foundations and began debates which continue to run, among people who are quite unaware of their origins. The Unit's location within NIACE provided a solid administrative foundation and linkage into the many networks which the Institute touched. During its existence NIACE itself was transformed, and has taken the agenda of broadening the concern for adult learning into all corners of society, forward with vigour. The battle continues!

Stephen McNair

Stephen McNair worked for the WEA in West Sussex, moving successively to the Local Education Authority there, and to Essex LEA. He came to NIACE in 1984 to be Head of UDACE, and became Director of Research in 1992, upon the Project's conclusion. The UDACE record is one of impressive teamwork allied to Stephen's 'workaholicism' noted by Don Grattan, UDACE's first Chairman. Stephen was appointed Head of the School of Education Studies, at Surrey University, in 1998.

A BROADCASTER'S PERSPECTIVE

Don Grattan

Television and the education of adults – the 1960s

E DWARD HUTCHINSON'S name appears in so many places in any account of the evolution of education for adults but, in danger of being overlooked, is Edward's concern for the role of that broadcasting could play.

BBC national radio had been making a contribution for some years but it was the publication of the Pilkington report in 1962, followed by the Government White Paper, that securely established for the first time an obligation on the broadcasters to set aside time for specialised broadcasts in the field of education for adults.

The White Paper proposed that additional hours of television (above the 50 hours per week allowed by regulation) should be permitted. This meant that 'educational programmes for adults' had to be defined for the purpose of approval by the Postmaster General.

This was the origin of the celebrated definition, which was first composed by John Scupham of the BBC in consultation with Jo Weltman of the ITA and Edward Hutchinson of the NIAE.[1]

This definition – and the later modernised version – has been swept away by events such as the abandonment of restricted hours and a much more flexible and informed attitude as to what education for adults now embraces.

---

1   More details of may be found in *Learning over the Air* by John Robinson.

The first definition? *Educational television programmes for adults are programmes (other than school broadcasts) arranged in series and planned in consultation with appropriate bodies to help viewers towards a progressive mastery or understanding of some skill or body of knowledge.*

Edward's advice to the broadcasters both on educational priorities and 'Appropriate Bodies' was invaluable.

'On the move' – broadcasting, cash and the adult literacy programme

It was in July 1974 that Arthur Stock, Director of the NIAE, telephoned my office in the Langham Hotel where the BBC housed the small head-quarters unit for educational broadcasting. My secretary reported that Arthur Stock would be coming by at about 2 o'clock and he proposed that the two of us should go to the DES at Elizabeth House next to Waterloo Station in order to meet the Assistant Secretary who held the purse strings for educational research. In the taxi, Arthur and I polished our 'back-of-envelope' figures and I said that the BBC Education Departments had set aside £800,000 for a three-year project as a contribution to our national broadcasting campaign in the field of adult literacy. What was needed additionally was a sum of about £200,000 for what could be described as 'non-broadcast' activities.[2] These included a modest bid for funds to mount a respectable research project over and above the somewhat generalised audience research which the BBC would undertake anyway.

During that short taxi ride I briefed Arthur more fully on the BBC's intentions while he briefed me on the subtleties of negotiating with the Department's researchers. 'Just tell them how much you will be spending,' said Arthur. I dutifully did this and became aware that our intended contribution flabbergasted them. History shows that the Department came up with £45,000 for research and this sum was administered by the NIAE

---

2   More details of this may be found in *Adult Literacy and Broadcasting* by David Hargreaves, Producer of the television series, *On the Move*.

with a project under the supervision of Henry Arthur Jones, Professor of Adult Education at the University of Leicester.

The birth of UDACE

Way back, the publication of reports about the need for increased resources always seemed to lead to 'pigeon holes', disappointment and disillusionment. The Russell Report (1973) contained a central recommendation for the establishment of a National Council for Adult Education. Many of us thought that we could well be on our way!

At the end of 1977 the 'way' became the ACACE. Brilliantly chaired by Richard Hoggart, it had no real money but some lively sparks in membership. We reported to the DES early in 1982 and we waited, watching the political clouds all the while.

Arthur Stock, NIACE's assessor to the Council, beavered away seeking to convert 'policies into practice' by persuading the DES to fund a development body or council. Eventually, we were to hear that the Department would agree to finance a very small development unit. Arthur approached me to chair the proposed unit and, although I thought the budget was hideously small, I provisionally agreed.

To my dismay I was to learn that Alan Tuckett, undoubtedly one of the liveliest practitioners in adult education and a skilled orator, had publicly scorned the idea because of the inadequate funding and had proposed that the Institute should have nothing to do with it.

As I say, I was dismayed by this report and momentarily hesitated. However, UDACE was created with a mini-budget and we were able to appoint Stephen McNair as Head of the Unit.

I don't think we ever looked back. Stephen – a splendid workaholic – provided the informed and committed leadership that was essential. Alan Tuckett (who had joined the Unit's Steering Committee in 1986), now appointed Director of NIACE, could not have been more encouraging and supportive; although UDACE was wound up in its existing form in 1992, many of the policies it advocated with the backing of the Institute have now come to fulfilment. Alan survived the lean years – full marks for that!

Don Grattan

Don Grattan was Controller of Educational Broadcasting for the BBC, a member of the Advisory Council for Adult and Continuing Education (ACACE) and the first Chair of UDACE – Unit for the Development of Adult Continuing Education. One of his colleagues was John Robinson, whose book, 'Learning Over Air' discusses the role of broadcasting and the education of adults. NIACE awards a periodic bursary to educators, in memory of John Robinson.

ROLLING BACK THE
DARK CLOUDS

ADULTS AND HIGHER EDUCATION: THE NIACE ROLE?

Stephen McNair

NIACE HAS ALWAYS had an ambivalent relationship with Higher Education. Academics specialising in the education of adults have played a major part in the Institute's work, informing, contributing and steering its progress and development. The Institute has maintained close links with HE staff whose specialism is in the education of adults. However, the HE agenda has never been central to NIACE, just as the adult agenda has never been central to mainstream Higher Education. The underlying tension, between a respect for academic knowledge and values, which at times became a kind of intellectual deference, and a desire to transform HE in the interests of adult learners and potential learners, can be seen through much of the Institute's history. Since the mid-1980s, as lifelong learning, and adult learners specifically, rose in policy prominence this underlying tension has come more sharply into focus.

Although many of the great Civic Universities had their origins in serving the needs of their local communities and in the education of adults, most evolved after the second World War into publicly-funded institutions teaching a fiercely selected five per cent of school leavers, all studying full-time in residence. Alongside this mainstream, adult learners in Universities were the preserve of 'extramural' departments, which provided for those 'beyond the walls' of the real institution in the R.H. Tawney tradition. As their roots in a pre-war compensatory tradition whose rationale was challenged by the arrival of universal secondary schooling, such Departments cultivated a diverse set of traditions and values. In a few, accredited courses were offered – notably at London, Manchester and Nottingham. However, the majority of Departments created programmes of liberal, non-award-bearing, student-centred, community-based, locally-delivered activity which increasingly marked them apart from the mainstream of their host institutions.

In the late 1960s the focus began to change. The concerns for social equity which saw the expansion of adult education generally also led to the creation of the Open University, offering a radical view of how the 'higher' learning needs of adults could be met, and influencing a generation of teachers who worked for it part-time, alongside work in other HE and FE institutions. It also saw the rise of the Polytechnics, whose more vocational and part-time curriculum involved many adults, who were usually seen simply as more students: perhaps attending part-time alongside full-time young people, but not requiring, as a group, distinctive treatment. A broader concern for social equity led to the growing debate on expansion of HE, and of adult participation, and the beginnings of the access movement, which gathered pace in the 1980s.

The 1980s saw Government taking a firmer control of the funding, and of the policy agenda, of HE. Its concern about economic competitiveness led to specific initiatives in vocational education and continuing professional development (CPD) for adults, and the removal of restrictions on student recruitment which led to spectacular expansion of the whole system. Alongside this, adult participation grew rapidly, with the proportion of mature students in HE increasing by nearly 60 per cent, over the decade. At the end of the 1980s, for the first time, there were more mature students than school-leavers in British HE, and they remained a majority into the new century.

The 1990s brought major structural change. The division in titles and funding between Universities and Polytechnics was abolished, and with it the separate funding for extramural departments, leading to major reappraisal of their role and programmes. Government became interested in widening access, and the Funding Councils began to intervene with special initiatives designed to achieve this. To secure funding from a more utilitarian paymaster, most extramural departments made a major shift from non-award-bearing to accredited programmes. NIACE welcomed the attention to adult learners, but was anxious, along with its allies in the extramural world, both about the loss of a distinctive liberal tradition and the need to protect informal, community-based initiatives.

The Dearing Committee on Higher Education recommended reform of student funding and widening of adult and part-time access, and pointed out that the expansion of the system from five per cent to 33 per cent of school-leavers had produced almost no change in the social composition of the student body. Dearing did not, however, comment strongly on the inequity of financial support for part-time students, who were not eligible for the financial support offered to their younger peers. It is significant that the Government decision, post-Dearing, to remove maintenance grants and introduce of fees for full-time undergraduates was publicly perceived as abolishing 'free access' to HE: something which most mature students had never had.

As a champion of 'adult' learning, NIACE has always had a strong sympathy with those in HE who argued for the distinctiveness of adults, and hence their separateness, in structural and curricular terms. It was from this separate base that the extramural world brought about significant curricular innovations: they played a major part in creating fields like Local History and Women's Studies, and exploring and developing new models of delivery like the access course, and programmes for trades unions. For this reason, the Institute maintained close working relationships with the Extramural Departments, and many of their leaders played key roles in its work.

However, the Open University, which rapidly became the largest HE institution in the country, and the developing Polytechnics, challenged the notion that a separate position in mainstream institutions was the only, let alone the best, way to provide for adults. During the 1970s and 1980s the extramural world came to seem more marginal, both to the new forms of adult learning which were emerging – in FE, the Local Authorities – and to HE, where adult participation was expanding through CPD programmes and adult participation in Polytechnics, with whom NIACE had traditionally weaker links.

Two NIACE reports symbolise the tension. In 1989, *Adults in Higher Education* took the 'respectful' view of HE, arguing for equity for adults in an expanding, but fundamentally unchanged system. Four years later *An Adult Higher Education* took a more challenging position: arguing that the rise of lifelong learning, and the new dominance (numerically but not culturally) of adult learners called for a reappraisal of the purposes and structures of the whole system. The paper proposed that HE should recognise the lifelong perspective by becoming more student-centred, economically and socially engaged, explicit about processes and out-comes, and less socially exclusive. It proposed a reshaping of structures around learner support (to make an individualised and flexible curricu-lum possible), curriculum reform (providing a more coherent founda-tion for all 'graduates', an equitable geographical coverage and strategies for negotiation and empowerment); and a credit framework (making it easy for individuals to combine learning undertaken at different times and with different providers).

An Adult Higher Education was warmly received in institutions and among policymakers, but subsequent attempts to follow through some of its more radical implications ran into real resistance. Its curricular argu-ments, for example, implied that public resources would be more equi-tably used if those currently deployed to provide a minority with three years' full-time HE were redirected. This would give a larger proportion of the population access to a shorter, more generic 'foundation' experi-ence of HE, as a jumping-off point for lifelong learning. This idea was being discussed in several quarters, but ran into two distinct kinds of opposition: from those defending what had been achieved for (a minority of) adult learners, and from those defending the three-year Honours degree as the irreducible core of a proper HE. Both implied that equity could only be achieved through greater Government investment, which did not come, and when Government finally accepted the argument, its 'Foundation Degree' was a minor and marginal new set of specific voca-tional programmes, delivered largely outside Universities through FE col-leges. The fundamental challenge to the mainstream had been evaded.

The example illustrates some of the tensions inherent in the relation-ship. NIACE's agendas touch on very different, and sometimes conflicting, parts of the HE system. Each of the four groups of 'adults' in higher education identified in *An Adult Higher Education* ('deferred beginners', 'returners', 'developers' and 'enrichers') has distinct needs from higher education, and all are marginal to the mainstream agendas of universities and other HE institutions. The Institute's traditional commitment to social inclusion pulls against some of the most powerful cultural forces of HE, whose concern to maintain quality can sometimes manifest itself in social (and age-based) exclusivity. NIACE challenges the sector to think more widely about its role as a lifelong model of learning establishes itself, and HE challenges NIACE to think rigorously about the nature of adult learning. As HE becomes more vocationally relevant, NIACE worries about the loss of curiosity-led pursuit of knowledge, of the liberal tradition, and the needs of those who do not seek to be economically active, including the growing retired population.

For HE, accustomed to a dominant position in the status hierarchy of English education, the interface with other sectors is a minor concern. For NIACE, concerned with how the total system serves adult learners, this issue is central, and one which sometimes puts the Institute in tension with its HE members. NIACE also has to struggle with the tension between integration and separation: would adult learners be better served by special 'adult' or 'access' institutions, which could respond better to their particular needs (if their needs are really distinct)? Or would a more 'diverse' system of HE inevitably mean the rise of 'second class' institutions for the adult, part-time and 'non-traditional'?

Stephen McNair

Stephen McNair worked for the WEA in West Sussex, moving successively to the Local Education Authority there, and to Essex LEA. He came to NIACE in 1984 to be Head of UDACE, and became Director of Research in 1992, upon the Project's conclusion. The UDACE record is one of impressive team work allied to Stephen's 'workaholicism' noted by Don Grattan, UDACE's first Chairman. Stephen was appointed Head of the School of Education Studies, at Surrey University, in 1998.

INTERNATIONAL ASPECTS AND
EXCITING DEVELOPMENTS: 1975−1995

Howard Fisher

TODAY NIACE BASKS deservedly in the reflected glory of the first
International Learners' Week launched in Germany, in September
2000. At the same time the latest Annual Report from the Institute
emphasises the extensive and solid depth of its international collaboration, not just in nearly all parts of Europe, but throughout the world via
the networks of the ICAE, and, even more significantly, UNESCO itself.

When I joined the Institute in 1975 from an area organiser's post in
the West Midlands to help start up the ALRA, I saw immediately that
there was an important international dimension to the Institute's work,
despite its extremely limited resources. In just a small office in Central
London, with single-figure staff, and a turnover of scarcely £100,000, (in
contrast to today's expanding Leicester-based organisation where the
wages bill now exceeds £1m) the Institute already had an international
reputation. A steady stream of overseas visitors came to its modest
library. This was undoubtedly due, as so often, to the power of the English language, which had been a factor in the formation of the World
Association of Adult Education in 1919, even before the founding of our
predecessor, the BIAE in 1921, following the Ministry of Reconstruction's
Report on Adult Education in 1919. The Institute's main journal, *Adult
Education*, was sold in A5 format to over 50 countries and *Studies in the
education of adults*, which came later, was read by academics and leading practitioners in every continent.

Edward Hutchinson, Secretary of the NIAE, had not immediately
rushed to join the European Bureau of Adult Education, set up in the

Netherlands under the leadership of Bob Schouten, a charismatic figure. However, by 1963 Edward had been persuaded to undertake what turned out to be a ten-year term as President of the Bureau. Many foundation stones were laid that far back which now support NIACE's impressive European reputation today because – despite the occasional spat and personality clash – at least in adult education circles 'everyone liked the English; we all trusted the Brits'.

In 1971 Arthur Stock came to head the Institute following Edward's retirement; he continued to pursue a steady international line, with the occasional risky flourish. In 1972 UNESCO held its third World Conference on Adult Education. As usual most of the delegates were representatives of national governments, but with a small cohort of recognised NGO personnel. At this event in Tokyo, Arthur Stock met the internationally-renowned Roby Kidd. From their speculative late-night discussions came the proposals for the International Council for Adult Education. This was an attempt to give the several and scattered non-governmental adult education organisations, worldwide, a more influential voice in UNESCO. Roby Kidd managed to find some Canadian Government money, and eventually secured a Kellogg Foundation contribution from the United States. Helmuth Dolff, the German President of the EBAE, was instrumental in persuading the Bureau to support the ICAE idea.

Since such small beginnings, from more than a generation ago, the National Institute has been able to participate in major ICAE events in Jamaica, France, Thailand, Argentina and elsewhere, and in subsequent UNESCO World Conferences. NIACE's influence has steadily increased as it has shared good UK practice and ideas with colleagues. Because of this, recent support for its proposal for an International Adult Learners' Week was almost a foregone conclusion.

I came to NIAE with some facility in French and German and thought I'd receive the bonus of a little sponsored foreign travel. However, my first international event was in this country in 1976! The theme, a topic of the moment, was *Provision for disadvantaged groups*. The venue, inappropriately enough, was a castle in Surrey. European Bureau delegates had come to hear about the amazing adult literacy campaign that had started the year before, with such support from the BBC's television series *On the move* with Bob Hoskins. They could scarcely believe that 100,000 students had come forward in the first 12 months; that almost 25,000 volunteers had offered their services without pay, to work under the supervision of a few full-time professionals.

The adult literacy campaign was a great boost to the prestige of the NIAE. It brought interest from the Out of School Division of the Council of Europe in Strasbourg. We just had to agree to their request for a study tour. In 1981 the International Council approached the Institute for a similar tour. Alan Wells from the ALBSU (ALRA's successor) joined forces with the Institute to organise another seminar called *Adult literacy in industrialised countries.* The theme continued to attract international attention: the European Bureau conference in 1983 at St. Andrew's University was co-hosted by NIACE and the now sadly defunct Scottish Institute of Adult Education. The guardianship of ALRA, and its successors, and the collaboration between it and the Institute in the development of major events, proved our credibility was impeccable.

During the 1980s the Institute was constantly engaged in international connections: the work of, and with, the European Bureau was particularly significant. Many topics were covered in international conferences, with major summer gatherings in Finland and Austria. Subjects included a pioneering occasion called *Women in adult education – learning new roles in a changing world.* Other topics included *Adult education and health, Paid educational leave* – important to European educators, and the beginning of a long series about the use, value and practicality of information technology in the education of adults.

Despite financial difficulties there was indeed, an international highlight every year. We had a remarkable exchange with China, although the first time round, the three-person delegation had to delay its departure for a year or so because of the demonstrations in Tiananmen Square on the timely intervention of the British Council.

International services had another dimension too. Its routine work was on going, not glamorous, but waiting to spot the openings, waiting and hoping for the days when subsidy and project money would flow freely. Every letter from abroad received a polite reply. Also included were those from enquirers who had found our name in an international directory and thought that the Institute was a teaching establishment offering certificates and diplomas! When we could, we sent out free copies of publications, usually by surface mail; correspondents were referred to colleagues we knew in their own countries. Typically, contact was made with more than 100 countries annually. At one time the International Council placed on record that NIACE was the only member organisation that had responded to every communication, every policy paper and every request mad by the Council for help and advice.

During the 1980s, both REPLAN, headed by Tony Uden, and UDACE, led by Stephen McNair, were able to involve an international dimension in the different roles they played. REPLAN secured some funding through the SOCRATES programme, and other European Community funds; UDACE developed an Organisation for Economic Co-operation and Development dimension (OECD), and involved the World Bank.

Some corporate members of the Institute strongly supported our international work. Both the WEA and the ECA backed NIACE in its endeavours. Further encouragement came from the Commonwealth Association for the Education and Training of Adults (CAETA). University Departments with connections in Australia and Africa had strong links with our objectives and us. The Commonwealth (formerly the Imperial) Relations Trust bursaries enabled recipients to travel abroad, and connect with the education of adults systems in many countries.

Alan Tuckett, Principal of the Clapham and Battersea Adult Education Institute, and previously Head of the Friends Centre in Brighton, became Director in 1988. He came as a ready-made internationalist, with a background of involvement in the International League for Social Commitment in Adult Education (ILSCAE). Under his leadership Adult Learners' Week developed in England and Wales, and spread to Europe and elsewhere through the international network. The Week happened almost by chance. This was the greatest boost of all. We'd heard about what the Americans did: logo bunting on every gasoline station, declarations by most of the States in favour of adult education, and award-winning adult learners having breakfast with their State Senators on Capital Hill. No one had actually seen all this. Martin Yarnit, of

Sheffield Metropolitan Authority, managed a detour during a transatlantic visit, and returned to suggest it was an idea that we might try. Alan confidently asserted that we should, and the rest is 'history', so fast and so far has the initiative and its spin-offs spread.

Today, everyone wants to 'play' with NIACE; politicians of all shades, trades unions leaders, 'soap' celebrities, funding bodies and sponsors. Many countries have followed our lead. Many seek to stand on the platform that has been built. Much public support has been achieved. Events are moving so quickly that it is difficult to keep up with the Institute's dramatic progress.

Five years ago I retired from NIACE, but I do still remember those committed activists in Spain, Slovenia, and the Czech Republic and elsewhere in Europe and the world – the list is long! I think with affection of all the hard working, imaginative *animateurs* at home and abroad who helped in every part of my work over 20 years.

There is still so much to do for adult learners, internationally, and on the 'home patch'. I don't envy the new generation that has to put in so much more effort. I hope that they will continue to find the time and energy to maintain those increasingly important international links.

My best wishes to all.

Howard Fisher

Howard Fisher was Associate Director of NIACE from 1975 to 1995. His tenure spans both the move from London to Leicester, and from 19b De Montfort Street, to next door at No. 21.

GROWING INDEPENDENCE IN WALES
NIACE DYSGU CYMRU

Howard Gilbert and Dewi Jones

WELSH PEOPLE HAVE always had a profound belief in, and respect for, education. Today there are 46 colleges of further education, and 23 university colleges in the Principality. Adult education in particular has featured strongly. In recent years the Valleys Initiative for Adult Education, fostered and encouraged by Professor Hywel Francis, a Vice-President of NIACE, has breathed life into the framework of community centres, colleges, and residential adult education, that have long been at the heart of the services.

NIACE connection with Wales, through its forebear the BIAE, goes back to the foundation of Coleg Harlech in 1927 and its President, Lord Haldane. That link persisted in the person of Dr. Thomas Jones, co-founder and first Chairman of Governors. He ended a distinguished civil service career as Deputy Secretary to the British Cabinet, serving first Lloyd George, then Bonar Law and Stanley Baldwin, and finally Ramsey McDonald. Later he became President of Coleg Harlech and, in 1930, Secretary of the Pilgrim Trust which – at the outset of the second World War – brought him into a close partnership with W. E. Williams (then Secretary of the BIAE), and to become a founding member of the CEMA, a war-time sub-committee of the BIAE Council and, ultimately, the embryo of the Arts Council.[1] Dr. Jones, an early student of University College, Aberystwyth, became its President from 1944 to 1954, spending many of his retirement years in the town. It is an historically fascinating quirk of fate that Jones' recorder in the *Dictionary of National Biography* is Ben Bowen Thomas. He too was a high-ranking civil servant; formerly a tutor at Coleg Harlech in his younger life, he served the Ministry of Education and, on retirement, became President and Chairman of Executive for the NIAE during Edward Hutchinson's tenure. NIACE has had a long connection with Wales and Welsh adult education.

Developments since the late 1970s have strengthened the ties between the Institute and the Welsh adult education community. Realisation of need, and growing strength for Welsh devolution, brought about the creation of NIACE's Welsh Committee in 1985 – a sub-group of the Executive which, in the late 1908s, became a fully-fledged unit with an office in Cardiff and the title 'NIACE Cymru' (from 1988), under the guidance of Anne Poole, Associate Director, NIACE. Recently that movement has been further strengthened with the creation of NIACE Dysgu Cymru (NIACE Learning Wales) in 2000. This change is in line with the new National Assembly's responsibility through its Post-16 Committee for the education and training of adults in the Principality.

The changes wrought by the Assembly, the establishment of a single framework for all post-16 education and training, a single inspectorate, and an accreditation and qualifications system, is a culmination of long-wished for circumstances in which the rich diversity of the Welsh post-16 education system could, nevertheless be provided with a coherent framework that would offer 'clear stepping stones to achievement for learners whatever their ages'. (Reynolds, in *Adults Learning*, March 2001). To illustrate this great quality of Welsh education – with its roots in church and chapel, and the closeness of community life – Dewi Jones, Honorary Life Member of NIACE and former Assistant Education Secretary to the Welsh Joint Education Committee (WJEC), provided a NIACE conference with an exciting view of its complexity, quality and kaleidoscopic character. He foreshadows much of what has recently happened, and is continuing.

1　Refer also to Part 1: The Origins of NIACE

Adult education in Wales: a complexity of collaborations

Whatever your imagination, or stereotype, of Wales is, whether it be a declining post-industrial valley community, or the lonely shepherd on a wind-swept hillside, I am sure there is an appropriate example. However, if you wish to begin to understand Wales and its people it is important to grasp a fundamental fact: Wales is a country of great heterogeneity, it is a complicated place. Not only is the north different from the south but, more significantly, the east from the west, and within relatively small areas there are marked social, economic and linguistic differences. There is, of course, another major chasm, Welsh-speaking/non-Welsh-speaking; others include chapel/church, the developing coastal towns with their marinas and yachts as second homes; the changing towns of the valleys where some struggle to buy first homes costing less than £10,000 and the relatively prosperous market towns of inland Wales adjusting to the effects of the second agrarian revolution.

Labour heartlands, Tory safe seats, rebellious nationalists, a Welsh-speaking establishment heavily influencing our educational system, co-existing uneasily with a dominant political establishment – certainly a complicated place.

Welsh adult educators are very aware of the opportunities and challenges this heritage and set of circumstances present. There have been many issues for adult educators to face and it is possible to identify certain trends in the way adult education has developed in the Principality. Here I highlight three, conceding that there may well be others of equal importance.

Clients at the centre: the new (undivided?) orthodoxy

The first of the three is a discernible shift, over the last five years, from a mainstream, demand-led service to a needs-based, client-centred service, using a wider range of methods to involve individuals and groups in learning. The new curriculum bears little resemblance to the old. It is characterised by 'empowerment', helping people to gain knowledge and skills that will give them greater control over their lives. Those benefiting are often unaware that they are recipients of education and in view of the disservice done to them by initial education it is often best that this remains the case.

Two issues spring from this change in practice. The first is the continuing use of increasingly inappropriate criteria for recognising good practice. Sadly some senior officers and also some elected members are still wedded to the 'turnstile mentality' – numbers, whether of classes or students, still remain the supreme measure of success. Breaking this mindset will be difficult, but it is happening.

Another issue arising out of this first trend is the confusion that seems to centre over the increasing use of the term 'community education'. There are innumerable definitions often competing with one another. The immediate danger is that we are beginning to hear the term applied in an exclusive way to the 'needs-based' activities referred to earlier. Helping a tenants' association – community education; working with an unemployed self-help group – community education; setting up local history projects that bring together older adults and children – community education. The danger is most manifest when these activities are presented as the proper preserve of the 'community educator' with the implication that the adult educator should stick to the old model of mainstream provision. A strategy of community education can and should encompass many areas of education; it should encourage overlap and integration and, in adult education terms, facilitate needs-based responses. However, we must resist those who wish to create new specialisms and, as a consequence, new divisions. FE/AE is bad enough, surely we do not want AE/CE (or YE/CE)?

Therefore adult education, dominated by Monday to Thursday 7.00 to 9.00 pm, seems increasingly to be the old model. Monday to Sunday 18 hours a day, everyday, seems to be the new; a practice to which more and more of us aspire. Adult educators are feeling less constrained by roles and structures designed in another age, and are increasingly encouraged to disregard the institutional parameters that have bound so many of us in the past. Taking skills and services to where they are required, shaped by the needs of adult learners, this must be the new orthodoxy.

Collaboration: an added value

The question also arises of collaboration: collaboration between adult education services and between adult education and complementary services. National bodies have had a part in this, the WJEC REPLAN network, the NIACE staff development project and NIACE Cymru itself have undoubtedly facilitated the development of effective networks. This national activity has established a recognisable pattern of interaction, but it is at regional and neighbourhood level that we see evidence of concrete collaborative work. The Valleys Initiative for Adult Education, directed by Hywel Francis, is a good example, with echoes of the Russell Report's local development council. Seeking to reach people who usually miss out, the scheme also aims to harness the education of adults in support of community development and socio-economic re-generation.

The Initiative involves three LEAs, the WEA, the OU and two extra-mural departments and a host of diverse voluntary and community groups. If you examine documentation associated with this work you will be heartened to see words and phrases such as 'needs-based', 'linking to community development' and 'empowerment', and the acceptance that 'adult educators are themselves learners'. This is just one of the many examples of the powerful 'added value' that collaboration can bring. The lesson is increasingly understood and exhibited throughout Wales.

Language matters

The third trend is the increasing profile of the Welsh language and the realisation that for adults to learn the language effectively they need a style of provision that is concentrated, multifaceted in technique and dependent on good continuing support. This area is topical and controversial. The proposal for teaching Welsh to adults centred on a series of full-time centres in every LEA and totalled £800,000 in the first year, rising in succeeding years to £2m and £3m. The total cost for the four-year plan would have been £8m. It would not be appropriate to become embroiled in the controversy, but you might be interested to know that the demand from adults – including English settlers wishing to learn the language – is huge. Recent research showed that up to 700,000 adults wished to learn the language. Should these actually press for tuition 99 per cent would have to be turned away. No wonder that leading practitioners are reticent about promoting the language.

The question of attitudes to the language is complicated and emotional, but there is an increasing awareness of the benefits in cultural and economic terms that accrue from its mastery. Perhaps the most significant force in Welsh education is the rapid expansion in the number of Welsh-language secondary schools. A growth that would be greater if increased provision were not dependent on demonstrable demand – ABE practitioners and guidance workers will recognise the point. Graduates of these schools are the adults of tomorrow, with obvious implications for our service. Many of their parents – monoglot in the majority – wish to learn Welsh and are effectively prevented from doing so by the lack of available services.

An additional complication for us, and readers working in areas of England with high immigrant populations might also identify with this, is that we have to address a quickly-changing social, cultural and linguistic scene. The rate of immigration into our country areas, formerly strongholds of the language, grows apace. The social structures of long-standing communities are changing. The potential for division and strife is apparent. Adult educators have an honourable tradition for social action and for us in Wales the time to re-discover this characteristic has arrived. We need to work with others to encourage tolerance, to display the richness that comes from the co-existence of a diversity of cultures.

An environment for adult learning

The trends mentioned are obviously not developing in a vacuum, but are affected by various forces. Some of these are potentially devastating and could endanger much of what we hold dear.

This sense of urgency and an appreciation that the future will increasingly belong to those who can and will demonstrate self-determined success must also be exhibited by us as adult educators. Therefore, adult education will need to develop a variety of methods to build support. Where it needs to be strengthened, where it is absent, do something about it today – tomorrow may well be too late. Consider the following examples of diversity. In the docklands of Cardiff a supplementary school for black children run on Saturday mornings provided the catalyst for a black women's group. It struggles to establish itself. In a leafier part of Wales another adult education activity – a prestigious international celebration of the work of Dylan Thomas – was understandably oversubscribed. Both are valid and valuable parts of the adult education scene in Wales.

Existing organisations will give a different priority to such interests. Their different methods of facilitating the education of adults must be preserved and developed, not in a competitive 'me and my organisation first' environment, but in one where the adult educator can be at ease in supporting and furthering the cause of adult learning wherever it takes place.

DRAMA, GROWTH AND FUN ...
NIACE IN THE 1990S

Judith Summers

T O R E F L E C T on the last 15 years of NIACE's story, during which I was an actor rather than observer, means offering a personal view of some major themes in a dramatic and often turbulent time of change for adult learning and (therefore) for NIACE. In the ten years from 1990 to 2000, core staff numbers grew from 22 to 76, and income from £638,090 (excluding the units) to £3,534, 208 (excluding grants distributed)[1]. The range of its interests and membership has increased accordingly. But the success the figures suggest has not come easily, and part of the fascination of the period has been that the definition itself of 'success' is a matter of debate.

The heart of the matter

NIACE's understanding of its mission has, I think, been reinvented. It is not so much that we have tried to put adult learners first, as that we have at once broadened our recognition of who and where adult learners are, and held to the view that those who benefit least and encounter the greatest barriers deserve most attention. This was neither an obvious nor an uncontested route for the organisation to take, not least because it could offend institutional interests.

In 1991, NIACE published *Learning and Leisure* (Sargant, 1991), a study using a national survey of 4,600 adults conducted exactly ten years

---

1   Annual Report and Accounts for 1989/90 and 1999/2000.

after the ACACE Survey of 1980. The survey was timed to mark the ending of the ILEA and its adult education service, by providing a 'historical benchmark' of the service. It did more than demonstrate what was lost with ILEA; it was the first of a series of reports commissioned by NIACE through the 1990s which have demonstrated the fundamental and continuing 'learning divide' for adults (Sargant *et al*, 1990). Alongside the research, and growing out of the work of the three Equal Opportunities Committees in the 1980s and of REPLAN, came a wealth of publications and projects which explored both the theoretical basis and interventionist strategies in the interests of excluded groups. Issues of gender, race, class and age were explored and a substantial body of work on learning difficulties and disabilities developed. The title of *Education's for other people* (McGivney, 1990), one of the first, is a phrase which has taken on its own life, just as NIACE's summing up of the learning divide, 'if at first you don't succeed you don't' (Uden, 1990) has been widely quoted in policy discussions.

The cumulative impact of these studies has been huge. By showing that participation is consistently structured, they raised inescapable questions about equity and the right to learn, and created an agenda to which others had to respond: would the issue have been recognised anyway? Of course – but the research contextualised and helped to legitimate local effort, and provided the basis for national policy development, most notably in the work of the Kennedy Committee (the FEFC Committee on Widening Participation).

Funding for research and development flowed from both government and independent sources, including essential support from charitable foundations: widening participation was a winner. NIACE has not (yet) succeeded in creating the political will to tackle all the issues: but the respect paid to participation in the agenda for the new LSCs and lifelong learning partnerships, as compared to the 1991 White Paper, shows how far we have come – and I think NIACE can take some credit for this.

Although the closure of REPLAN, the absorption of UDACE into the FEDA, and the separation of the BSA from NIACE were experienced as heavy blows, I believe that each event liberated NIACE. The agencies' agendas became NIACE's own (although it was only in 1999 that NIACE formally confirmed its interest in basic skills as part of the wider agenda for participation[2]). Rapidly, NIACE worked to extend its sectoral spheres of influence. For example: it supported and popularised the idea of 'employee development' pioneered in the Ford Employee Development and Assistance Programme (EDAP); it produced an early study of adult learners in further education colleges (McGivney, 1991); it initiated work with dispossessed young adult learners. Progressively through the 1990s, NIACE could claim to speak with credibility on adult learning wherever it was.

The tensions which this produced were considerable. Executive members (and staff) worried, with some justice, about being over-stretched. But the real issues for debate concerned relations with government and fears of mission drift.

Working with government: inside or outside the tent?

I have no intimate knowledge of NIACE's working relationship with government in the 1980s. It felt very typical of how the establishment worked, and certainly deferential in public. The critical moment came in 1991. The White Paper, which did not quite write local authorities out of the equation, had just been published (HMSO, 1991). A review of NIACE's funding from central government in this context caused some panic. The outcome, scary at the time, was good. Rather than simply getting core funding, NIACE would receive its grant through a service-level agreement for conferences, publications and so on. This improved the transparency of the relationship, freed NIACE to bid for work which clearly fell outside the contract, and effectively confirmed its independence.[3] To NIACE's credit, it did not back off from campaigning on the Further and Higher Education Bill, as part of a coalition ranging from NATFHE (the further and adult education lecturers' union) to the National Federation of Women's Institutes (NFWI). There were some bad

2   Minutes of the NIACE Executive Committee Meeting of 24 June 1999
3   At the same time a public review by the Council for Local Education Authorities was very complimentary and recommended that funding by the Local Authority Associations should continue.

moments, summed up in the description of the coalition by the minister, Tim Eggar, as 'the forces of darkness'[4]. But the outcome was a grudging recognition in parliamentary debates that other elements of adult learning than the job-related mattered, and a formal safeguard in the Act.

Gradually, NIACE became skilled at handling the role of political criticism, and government came to accept the value of its independence. Of course the more conciliatory style and the genuine enthusiasm of ministers helped. But the extension of NIACE's interests, which I have described above, went hand-in-hand with the government's progressively widening agenda for lifelong learning. The concerns which this caused some members increased sharply after the change of government in 1997. 'Support' for the University for Industry (Ufi) was criticised – although here NIACE could better be described as contributing to debate. Could NIACE representatives both serve on Government Committees and retain their freedom to criticise (and indeed their primary obligation to NIACE)? The response to the 1999 Green Paper showed that they could[5]. Most recently the organisation has learnt to cope with the politics of seconding staff to work short-term with Government and other agencies, knowing that the results would be critiqued and criticised by the organisation itself.

Coping with the great divide: the system after 1993

The issue of 'mission drift' is more difficult. Had NIACE not engaged after the 1992 Further and Higher Education Act with the main national players such as the Further and Higher Education Funding Councils, it would have been marginalised and, I think, not long have survived: it would have been cut off from so much which affected adult learning. In engaging, it had to recognise where the participation agenda led: the valuing of all sorts and sites of adult learning, and not only 'liberal adult education'. Inevitably, this looked to some like support for the Government's competitiveness and employability priorities and for qualifica-

4   Quoted in *Education*, 13 December 1991
5   See *Adults Learning* of March and April 1998

tion-bearing courses at the expense of others. Members from the 'heart-lands' of adult education felt that it entailed neglect or disparagement of their work and made this clear; their feelings were not surprising in the context of the perceived marginalisation of non-accredited courses and heavy cuts in local authority spending. Alternatively, some argued that NIACE was simply losing the plot and failing to claim the space for more radical perspectives.

Accreditation became the centre of a sometimes bitter debate. UDACE, and then NIACE, has worked closely with the National Open College Network (NOCN) and supported the creation of adult-friendly accreditation. According to the 1992 Act, the FEFC was to fund qualifica-tion-bearing courses, with some exceptions; even where qualifications were not obligatory, for instance in basic skills, they were seen as proxies for quality and guarantors of progression. Similar movement took place in higher education. Faced with the double pressure of the FEFC funding regime and the cuts in LEA funding, or finding themselves on the wrong side of the divide, providers certainly adapted some courses unsympa-thetically. Some members argued that accreditation *per se* was inappro-priate to the aims of true adult education and learning for its own sake; or that 'the ultimate end of credentialism is that education becomes seen as nothing more than a preparation for work' (Marks, 2000). Others saw 'a tension between accreditation and widening access' and argued that for those taking the first steps in adult learning accreditation was a deterrent and offered the risk of further failure (Coats, 2000).

NIACE chose to try to work with the grain of the system, and to find the spaces in which real gains could be made; it was an approach which left some people feeling stranded. And in taking on strategic tasks, it was bound to upset its own constituencies from time to time. For example, when NIACE evaluated the Higher Education Funding Council's devel-opment programme for non-award bearing courses, its criticism was seen by some as politically unhelpful. Moving from acting as an advocate for members to advocacy for the field as a whole is hard.

Public visibility and fun

Nobody could argue that Adult Learners' Week has been other than a success. Starting in 1992, the Week has grown to a massive operation, with a full-time campaigns and promotions team, an estimated more than 100,000 people involved in events, wide media coverage, offshoot 'sign up' campaigns in September and March, and re-invention round the world. It invented the national helpline for adult learning. In 1997, the fifth UNESCO international conference on Adult Education (Confintea) adopted the recommendation to develop an annual UN week for adult learning and this was launched in September 2000.

The Week brings out the inventiveness and fun in adult learning which might otherwise be obscured by institutional rigour. You could: learn on top of a bus; create a green man in the woods to burn at the end of the day; find out about the helpline through your giro cheque; and about local learning on your supermarket till receipt. It is salutary to remember that the idea of the Week was greeted with doubts: would enough people join in? Was it suitable to give awards to individuals? Yes, and yes, and the benefit in terms of public and political visibility is incalculable. In the week, politicians and managers can enjoy adult learning in an uncontroversial environment and do some learning themselves. Appropriately, out of the learners' voices heard in the awards ceremonies came the National Adult Learners' Forum in 1999, and this offers a model for local fora now that the LSCs are charged with listening to learners.

Launching the Week was a decisive moment: NIACE in effect shouted that it was a very public player and welcomed everyone to the party. I realise in reflecting on it how much the organisation has been prepared to take risks and how necessary this has been.

Coping with growth

The late 1980s seem now to have been a period of careful preparation and discrete internal modernisation. Support structures were developed and systematised and working across former internal boundaries grew: 'synergy' was a popular word. A key moment was the launch of *Adults Learn-*

ing in 1989, a statement of the intention to reach out actively to a widening constituency. NIACE became a company limited by guarantee in 1991 and has gone through two revisions of its committee structures. The second, and more radical, followed the logic of the incorporation and removed some accumulated constitutional confusion: the Council was abolished and replaced by biannual general meetings of members with the new Assembly as an open forum for policy discussion. Have these changes, as some feel, diminished democracy in what is, after all, a membership body? This question is faced by many voluntary organisations, who rely on professionals to run their business and need to find an accommodation between the forms of democracy and ways in which their members can engage.

The issues have been twofold: about working through the change in lay members' involvement from detailed to strategic roles, and recognising that active 'membership' might mean participating in other ways than through formal structures. Interest group networks such as the Local Education Authorities Forum for the Education of Adults (LEAFEA) and the newer Further Education Forum for the Education of Adults (FEFEA), or the annual Race Equality Conference, need to be heard. I suspect that NIACE is better at listening to its members than they know, but its particular form of democracy is clearly still evolving and will need to take on participation through the website; the activity of the website groups is growing fast.

As NIACE grew, the use of 'external' funding became another source of tension. What were the criteria for choosing to bid for and accept external funding? Could we recognise the opportunity costs of doing so? How did contract work line up with the mission? And did NIACE not find itself in the position of bidding in competition with its own members? Of course, these were valid and sometimes unanswerable questions. NIACE could not stand outside the 1990s contract culture; the beneficial result was that it removed dependence on any one source of funding and in that way increased our influence. And it enabled us to extend our reach into new ways of configuring adult learning. Work on 'learning communities', for instance, is growing in influence as perhaps the key informing idea for lifelong learning in community regeneration and well-being.

The growing pains of the transformation of the budget were hard for staff, and even more demanding has been the new role of administering major grant programmes – the ACLF (with the BSA), Project 1999 (one-off DfEE grants) the Basic Skills Community Fund and Laptops for Community Education (again with the BSA). NIACE, inevitably, becomes the target for criticism when terms of reference decided by others are constraining, or when applications are required yesterday (I have done it myself). The enormous benefits have been not only the creativity unleashed but also the re-connection of the organisation with the field and with new players and workers in it.

And next...

Through the period, the Local Government Association has been a major funder and support. Its most recent review of funding calls on NIACE to 'raise awareness among potential users of its services, including councils who are not at present education authorities, and 'do more to evaluate activities ... to show the impact achieved'.[6] This encouraging invitation to show how much and widely adult learning matters signals how far we have come.

However, 'lifelong learning' is also under attack. To be sure there are important debates about whether the notion itself is impossibly amorphous and collapses purposeful, structured learning into normal human behaviour – so that it is unhelpful and offensive to speak of 'non-learners', even as a shorthand[7]. Different in kind is the sort of attack launched by the former head of Ofsted on lifelong learning as being 'more about utopianism than substance' and with the assumption that it is just another consumer choice[8]; or the assertion that it is a 'confidence trick' aimed at 'socialising individuals into accepting standard government perspectives (Füredi, 2001). NIACE, it seems, still has plenty to do in demonstrating that the structure of participation and exclusion it has revealed is

6 Report to the NIACE Annual General Meeting, October 2000 (unpublished)
7 See for example, Rogers, A. 'Learning: can we change the discourse?' in *Adults Learning*, January 1997
8 Quoted in *Adults Learning*, April 2000

not coincidental, and that learning is neither a consumer good nor a confidence trick, but a human right and one, essential means of solving our problems.

Judith Summers

Judith Summers joined the NIACE Executive in 1982 and was a member of the Women's Advisory Committee. She was Chair of NIACE from 1992 until 1999. She was also President of NATFHE (1990–1991) and a Vice-President of the European Association of Adults (1994–2001). She managed a district adult education service and then held senior posts in further education. Judith is now a consultant, mainly working with Cheshire County Council to coordinate its Lifelong Learning Development Plan, and with Cheshire Learning Partnership.

A RIGHT TO READ?

NIACE INVOLVEMENT IN 25 YEARS OF ADULT LITERACY IN THE UK

Alan Tuckett

L ITERACY HAS BEEN a site of social policy struggle in Britain for hundreds of years. On the whole the established order has been in favour of teaching reading, so people could follow written instructions and read improving texts. Dissenters have been more passionate about writing – to encourage people to share their own versions of reality. These themes recur in more recent debates generated since the launch of the UK Adult Literacy Campaign in the 1970s.

Public policy affecting adults in the United Kingdom with reading and writing difficulties seemed almost to be non-existent in Britain in the first half of the twentieth century. Indeed, since few people today are unable to recognise the word POLICE on a police car, or to write their names, the Government continues to report a nil percent return to UNESCO's enquiries about the scale of illiteracy in member states. Yet over recent years the figures accepted as the best available estimates of basic skills needs have risen steadily – from 1 million when the British Association of Settlements launched the Right To Read Campaign (BAS, 1974), to 3 million when the Advisory Council for Adult and Continuing Education reported on adult basic education in 1979 (ACACE, 1979) to 6 million in 1994, and as many as 7 million in the 1999 Moser Report, *A Fresh Start: Improving Literacy and Numeracy.*

Until the 1970s the major commitment to literacy work in Britain was found in institutions, notably the Army and the prison service. During the Second World War piecemeal arrangements were made, whilst 'the unfortunate illiterates continued to be a drag on the Army and on themselves, unable to read orders, to make the simplest application or report, or to correspond with their families' (Shawyer, 75). (Interestingly, women with basic skills needs were ineligible for recruitment to the women's armed forces throughout the war.)

From mid-1942 the Army began to make systematic provision, with the establishment of Basic Education Centres, with one instructor for every 10 to 12 men, in requisitioned houses, Nissen huts, in annexes in civilian schools, or in an Army Education Centre. Courses usually lasted six, and at most eight weeks full-time, and targeted the 'most intelligent' of each intake of Army conscripts with basic skills needs. 'A quite surprising number claim to have attended an ordinary school for the full nine years. A smaller number never attended at all, the majority of these being sons of gypsies, circus performers and other "travellers"'. (Shawyer, 79).

Attitudes

There was, nevertheless a widespread assumption in official circles that illiteracy was the fault of the person with the problem, and equated with a lack of intelligence. Shawyer comments, 'Needless to say the testimony of the illiterate regarding his childhood needs very careful sifting, for some of them tell incredible stories'. Attitudes changed slowly. The report of the first national survey of the extent of adult literacy undertaken in December 1971 by the National Association for Remedial Education commented:

> "*The personal immaturity, insecurity and impairment of social development associated with adult literacy is reflected in the number of men and women who either marry later or fail to marry …*
>
> *(L)ack of intelligence can be assumed to be a major factor associated with reading disability in adults. That about half of the students attending classes are deemed to be 'clearly of low intelligence' suggests that the community is always likely to include some persons of limited intellectual capacity who may nevertheless be functioning at or near their level of potential, even though their reading and writing abilities are sufficiently low to cause some personal embarrassment.'*
>
> (NARE, n.d., 4,6.)

Right to Read

The adult literacy campaign launched in the 1970s consciously rejected a model of literacy work built on 'Blaming the Victim', as Jane Mace described it in a memorable article (Mace, 1975):

> 'As tutors, we have no right merely to offer a second chance, a repeat performance of the teacher-pupil model that has already failed ... We have to shed the idea of superior versus inferior pupil, of the top stream teaching the bottom stream, of knowing teacher versus ignorant student ... It means, above all learning how to listen ... to give value and literate dress to an oral culture we have forgotten how to appreciate.'

The dominant energies in the subsequent 1975 campaign were concerned to give voice to students' own experiences, to use those experiences to produce texts that other literacy students might read and respond to. The aim was not to teach only common, or useful words, but powerful ones; to read the world, not just words.

The British Association of Settlements published the key campaign document, *A Right to Read* in May 1974, with a description of the size of the adult illiteracy problem, and a policy statement aimed at mobilising opinion and resources to eradicate the problem within a decade.

> 'The Government should enter into a firm commitment to eradicate adult illiteracy. There is no reason why it should be afraid of setting a target date, say 1985, by which time the incidence could be reduced to a fraction of its present level.'
>
> (BAS, 1974)

The Campaign had a powerful ally in the BBC, which decided to mount a major prime time broadcasting initiative to teach reading and writing. Together, they made literacy work publicly visible, and for the first time it was politically attractive to address the problem of educational failure.

A keen sense of timing affected the success of *A Right to Read*. The document was launched some 12 months before the BBC's ten minute, prime-time television series *On The Move* was to be shown. It was backed by a telephone helpline – time enough for Government to listen to the force of the arguments, and to act to support local providers in meeting the flood of demands for tuition expected when the programmes were shown. It is a mark of the success of BAS that the Government-funded programme should have been based so closely on its recommended strategy. A national Adult Literacy Resource Agency (ALRA) was established, as an Agency within the NIAE with a remit to strengthen teacher training, and to promote curriculum and materials development.

Its successors (ALU, ALBSU and the Basic Skills Agency) have continued and extended the work.

Much of the analysis in *A Right to Read* has, over the 25 years since the launch of the campaign, become common practice, but the tension between student-centred and institution-led programmes is always evident.

ALRA, ALU, ALBSU

The literacy programme in 1975–6 had many of the characteristics of a high-energy campaign, with vigorous debate amongst students, tutors and organisers about curriculum, pedagogy, skills and the politics of literacy. At the same time, local education authorities all over Britain were adjusting to a major expansion of provision, resulting from 50,000 people being referred by the helpline run in association with the BBC's programmes. Many made the case to Government that there was a need for full-time professional co-ordinators for adult literacy, and that there was clearly going to be a demand after the initial year. ALRA was given a renewed remit, again with £1 million a year, enabling the employment of staff who could be assigned to local authorities. The years 1976–8 brought the highest level of funding across the board dedicated to literacy work; and as the programme became embedded in local authorities' services, the vanguard influence of voluntary organisations began to diminish.

It was also during this time that the first of a number of questions into potential bias in written or printed materials used in literacy work was raised. After a public enquiry the same materials were published by the national agency as the best of good practice available – some illustration of the gap between continuing myths about literacy in the wider community, and the experience evolving in the Campaign. NIACE became directly involved in underpinning the Agency's role.

By 1978 with the end of major programming on the BBC, Government expected local authorities to take the funding of literacy work into their core programmes, and made adjustments to local government finance to take account of the increased expenditure. However, this funding of local authorities was not ring-fenced, and the overall local government rate support grant was cut in 1978–79.

Many literacy organisations were asked to take on a broader range of duties, and overall the platform of provision established in the first flush of the literacy campaign was at best maintained at the same level. Literacy programmes were now a normal, or as Paulo Freire might say domesticated, part of LEA adult education. The strength of this was that good programmes were able to offer coherent progression routes to other learning opportunities for students emerging from literacy provision; the weakness that some of the innovative fire of the first years of the programme was lost.

A period of uncertainty and turbulence followed, during which many initiatives were lost, but the influence of ALU, like ALRA, was disproportionate to its budget. It continued the practitioner-led and collaborative staff and curriculum development strategy, juggling this skilfully with the changing demands made by Government.

With the change of Government in 1979 this juggling became a more delicate task. The revised remit of the successor national agency, the Adult Literacy and Basic Skills Unit (ALBSU), reflected the changed priorities of a Government more concerned with problems of market failure than with the articulation of the voice of the dispossessed.

The insecurity of funding muffled debate about what a literacy programme was for, and whether we had enough of it. Radical literacy workers felt that they displaced opportunities for more fundamental debate on the causes of literacy problems, at least in the wider arena of public discussion.

Within the campaign, one of the striking successes of the work of the first decade was the development of a broad range of publications of adult students' writing. From *Fathers' Cap* (Cambridge House, 1986),

Brighton Writing to *Let Loose* and *I Wanted To Write It Down* and *A Bristol Childhood* (WEA), a distinctive range of working class voices spoke of the richness and complexity of experience given voice in literacy education. From a dearth of adult-centred material in 1975 there was, by the early 1980s, wide choice of writing powerful on its own terms. Central to this development was the national literacy student paper, *Write First Time*. The paper was managed by a collective of literacy practitioners, and edited each time from a different centre by a coalition of members of the collective, local organisers and students. Its funding relied, substantially, for most of its life on grants from the central agency. Its process of writing, editing, and publishing student experience broke new ground characteristic of Paulo Freire's ideas. By the early 1980s its direct, uncensored and critical voice led to conflicts with ministers, and after some delay, loss of its grant from ALBSU. This was not the first, or last, example of public conflict over the materials used in literacy education – nor were they limited to Tory administrations, as the recurrence of the debate in the Inner London Education Authority in the early 1980s showed.

The major innovation in national policy during the 1980s, however, was a concern to reshape the basic skills agenda to support the needs of the workplace. The Manpower Services Commission had, as part of its portfolio of measures to prepare people for industrial training, offered full-time TOPS Preparatory courses for unemployed adults seeking to improve skills in reading, writing, or in English language from the mid-1970s. At first these courses were for up to 36 weeks. They were welcomed, widely, and offered a key route to a second chance for beginning readers. Alas, as in so much of its policy thinking the MSC confused throughput with output, and steadily increased the numbers going through its courses, whilst at the same time shortening the maximum length of time it was possible to study, until by the mid-1980s courses of up to 13 weeks were only able to top-up skills for people narrowly failing the basic skills entry tests for vocational training.

Labour market conditions affected these changes. At the beginning of the 1980s Britain was in a recession, with large-scale youth unemployment, and rapidly growing unemployment. Whilst a 1981 report (MSC 1981) failed to recognise the needs for basic skills support at work, the

MSC's 1983 paper *Towards an Adult Training Strategy* recognised the case for special measures for people with 'particular needs' (whether resulting from disability, language needs, or basic skills), and the importance of access to information and advice for adults. The 1983 policy paper also recognised the importance of partnership between training and further and higher education bodies. This analysis was impressive, yet the action taken by Government did little to match it, as inadequate resources were committed for the scale of the demand. Access to basic skills work was in practice sketchy, and there was little co-ordination between Employment Department and DES planning affecting literacy and numeracy for adults, and little practical co-operation with ALBSU until the late 1980s.

Throughout the 1980s and 1990s Governments believed that the training of people in work should be the responsibility of employers, and that it should not be at the cost of the public purse. Yet for workers with basic skills problems, in a labour market where low-skilled jobs have disappeared rapidly, there has been little incentive to ask for employers' support. Building on pioneering work undertaken by the voluntary organisation Workbase, ALBSU launched a Basic Skills at Work initiative in the early 1990s to seek to overcome employer and worker resistance to addressing basic skills needs in work-based training programmes. A key element in successful intervention, as Workbase demonstrated, was the role of the education agency as a trusted honest broker, between workers and management, negotiating a programme based on careful needs analysis, and working outside conventional line management structures. A second part of the ALBSU strategy was to publicise the costs to British industry of not improving basic skills. ALBSU's estimate was that poor basic skills cost industry £5,000 million a year.

The Act of 1992

The 1992 Further and Higher Education Act was designed to bring some of the disciplines of the market to post-compulsory education. Responsibility for securing adequate academic, vocational and basic skills further education was transferred to new Further Education Funding Councils in England and Wales, though a major element of basic skills work continued to be provided by traditional adult education and community-based providers outside of the new college sector. Both as a result of Government pressure and student demand, provision across post-school education and training was increasingly certificated. Basic Skills was no exception to this, with ALBSU's introduction of competency-based Wordpower and Numberpower courses. The journey from the 1970s liberal and emancipatory curriculum to the skills and accreditation-based agenda of the 1990s is a long one – yet it is remarkable how effectively basic skills work was kept on the public policy agenda throughout the period.

However, not all the changes have addressed a narrowly work-related agenda. In the 1990s there has been a growth of work linking basic skills to work in health, to developments in tenant management of housing estates, and, with spectacular success, to family education. The Family Literacy initiative once again linked ALBSU with the BBC in a campaign to encourage parents to learn alongside their children. Following powerful and emotive advertisements on television 350,000 people rang for Family Literacy Packs, provoking a cash crisis in the Agency, but also contributing, at least in part, to the granting of a revised remit for the Agency. The renamed Basic Skills Agency is now to work across the age range – finally achieving a key recommendation of *A Right To Read* (1974).

The Moser Report

For 25 years a literacy campaign had succeeded in keeping the issue on the public agenda, but not to overcome the problem. The results of the 1997 International Adult Literacy Survey showed this graphically.

> '*Britain had 23% of adults with the lowest literacy levels, compared with three of our European partners: the Netherlands at 10%, Germany and Sweden each at 7%.*'
> (Source: Literacy Skills for the Knowledge Society. OECD, 1997)

A new Labour Government invited Sir Claus Moser to head a national inquiry, which led to the publication of a major report *A Fresh Start:*

Improving Literacy and Numeracy in 1999. The report proposed a national strategy for adult basic skills with ten main elements:

- National Targets
- An entitlement to learn
- Guidance, assessment and publicity
- Better opportunities for learning
- Quality
- A new curriculum
- A new system of qualification
- Teacher training and improved inspection
- The benefits of new technology
- Planning for delivery

To a considerable extent, its analysis is paralleled that of the *Right to Read* document. Like the earlier paper (1974), the Moser report 25 years later chose not to address the basic skills needs of adults with disabilities, or of people who speak English as an additional language. It did not focus on dyslexia. However, its critique was powerful. The report made clear the link between poverty and poor basic skills (and in particular between poverty and poor numeracy). It called for a massive injection of new funding, and a serious strategy for cutting by half the number of adults with literacy difficulties by 2010. The report envisaged an expansion of annual provision from 70,000 to 450,000 a year. More controversially, the report argued the case for the developments of national tests for literacy and numeracy, in the belief that these would motivate people with poor basic skills to take up study.

The Government warmly welcomed the report, without further consultation on the recommendations, and established a national basic skills support unit able to work across Government to prepare a national strategy for launch in the autumn of 2000. £20 million of new funding was announced, with the prospect of much more to follow. Yet it remains unclear how dramatically larger numbers of people with reading and writing problems, or with difficulties with number can be wooed to participation. It is likely that developments in discrete basic skills work will be accompanied by initiatives to embed basic skills support in all programmes of adult learning. It feels currently as if we are about to climb an important next step of the ladder. But overcoming a system that marginalised the poor and under-confident is a long-term task.

Alan Tuckett

Alan Tuckett, Director of NIACE, previously worked in Brighton and the ILEA. He is President of the Pre-school Learning Alliance and a Special Professor in Continuing Education at the University of Nottingham. He was Vice-Chair of the National Advisory Group for Continuing Education and Lifelong Learning, and advisors UNESCO on adult learning. Alan is a member of the Adult Learning Committee of the Learning and Skills Council.

Tail piece

"If we shadows have offended,
Think but this … and all is mended …
That you have but slumber'd here
While these visitors did appear.

And this weak and idle time,
No more yielding but a dream,
Gentles, do not reprehend;
If your pardon, we will mend.

And, as I'm an honest Puck,
If we have unearned luck,
Now to 'scape the serpent's tongue,
We will make amends ere long;

Else the Puck a liar call;

So farewell unto you all,
Give me your hands, if we be friends.

And Robin shall restore amends."

[Exit]

(A Midsummer Night's Dream, Act v, Scene 1,
W. Shakespeare)

REFERENCES

ACACE, (1979) *A Strategy for the Basic Education of Adults,* Leicester: ACACE

ACACE, (1982a) *Continuing education: from policies to practice: a report on the future development of a system of continuing education for adults in England and Wales,* Leicester: ACACE

ACACE (1982b) *Adults: their educational experience and needs: the report of a national survey,* Leicester: ACACE

ACACE (1983) *In the corners of our time: six years of the Council's work,* Leicester: ACACE

Beveridge, Sir W. (1942) *Social insurance and allied services,* London: HMSO

Board of Education (1943) *Educational Reconstruction,* London: HMSO

Brighton Writing, (1976) *Brighton Writing,* Friends Centre: Brighton

British Association of Settlements, (1974) *A Right to Read: Action for a literate Britain,* British Association of Settlements: London

British Institute of Adult Education, *Handbook and Directory (1928-29),* John Rylands Library, Manchester

British Institute of Adult Education *Minutes and proceedings 1934–1938,* NIACE Archive, Leicester

British Institute of Adult Education *Annual Reports 1939–1945,* NIACE Archive, Leicester

Brown, J.W. (1934) Haldane Memorial Trust Deed (J.W. Brown, Fund Treasurer) and witness W.E. Williams, NIACE Archive

Cambridge House Literacy Scheme Students, (1975) *Father's Cap and other stories,* Cambridge House: London

Clyne, P. (2000) 'Obituary: Lady Plowden', *Adults Learning,* Vol. 12 No. 2, Leicester: NIACE

Coats, M. (2000) 'Barriers and Building Blocks', *Adults Learning,* Vol. 11 No. 7, Leicester: NIACE

Coleg Harlech (1950) *Anniversary Publication* – 20 years, 1930–1950

Committee on Broadcasting (1962) *Report of the Committee on Broadcasting 1960 (Cmnd 1753)* (The Pilkington Report), London: HMSO

Department for Education and Employment (1998) *Accountability in further education: a consultation paper*, London: DfEE

Department of Education and Science (1973) *Adult education: a plan for development* (The Russell Report), London: Stationery Office

Department of Education and Science (1980) *Continuing education: post-experience vocational provision for those in employment*, London: DES

Department of Education and Science (1991) *Education and training for the 21st century*, London: HMSO

Dictionary of National Biography, Oxford: Oxford University Press

FEU/REPLAN (1985) *Adult unemployment and the curriculum: a manual for practitioners*, London: Further Education Unit

Fieldhouse, R (1996) *A History of Modern British Adult Education*, NIACE: Leicester

Füredi, F. (2001) quoted in 'We have ways of making you learn', *Times Higher Education Supplement*, 5 January.

Haldane, E. (1937) Haldane, Richard Burdon (Viscount Haldane, of Cloan), Dictionary of National Biography 1922–1930, 380–386, Oxford

Hall, B. and Stock, A. (1985) 'Trends in Adult Education since 1972', *Prospects: quarterly review of education*, Vol. 15 No. 1, UNESCO

Hargreaves, D. (1980) *Adult Literacy and Broadcasting: the BBC's experience – a report to the Ford Foundation*, London: Frances Pinter

Hoggart, R. (1957) *The use of literacy: aspects of working-class life with special reference to publications and entertainments*, London: Chatto and Windus

Houghton, Sir W. (1967) *The LEAs' response and responsibility.* In Hutchinson, E.M. (ed) (1971) *Aims and actions in adult education: 1921–71*, Leicester: NIAE

Hutchinson, E.M (1969) *Letters to Haldane Memorial trustees, and Official Custodian*, NIACE Archive, Leicester

Hutchinson, E.M (1986) *Biography of W E Williams* in Dictionary of National Biography, 1971–1980, 908–909: Oxford

Kennedy, H. (1997) *Learning works: widening participation in further education*, Coventry: FEFC

Legge, D. (1982) *The education of adults in Britain*, Milton Keynes: Open University Press

Leighton, B. (2000) 'NIACE 80th anniversary celebration in 2001', *Adults Learning*, Vol. 11 No. 7, Leicester: NIACE

Mace, J. (1975) *Blaming the Victim*, Times Educational Supplement, May 1975

Mace, J. (1979) *Working with Words: Literacy Beyond School*, Chameleon Writers and Readers: London

Manpower Services Commission, (1981) A New Training Initiative, MSC: Sheffield

Manpower Services Commission, (1983) *Towards An Adult Training Strategy*, MSC: Sheffield

Marks, A. (2000) 'The Paper Chase', *Adults Learning*, Vol. 11 No. 8, Leicester: NIACE

McGivney, V. (1990) *Education's for other people: access to education for non-participant adults*, Leicester: NIACE

McGivney, V. (ed) (1991) *Opening colleges to adult learners: report of the NIACE-TEED research project on adult learners in colleges of further education*, Leicester: NIACE

Ministry of Reconstruction (1919) *Final Report of the Adult Education Committee*. Cmd 321. HMSO

Moser, Sir Claus, (1991) *A Fresh Start: Improving Literacy and Numeracy*, HMSO: London

NAGCELL (1997) *Learning for the twenty first century: first report of the National Advisory Group for Continuing Education and Lifelong Learning*, London: DfEE

National Association for Remedial Education, Adult Illiteracy Sub-Committee (1971) *Adult Illiteracy*, NARE: Kingston Upon Hull

National Institute of Adult Education (1955) *Liberal education in a technical age*, London: Max Parrish

NIACE (1989) *Adults in Higher Education*, Leicester: NIACE

NIACE (1993) *An Adult Higher Education*, Leicester: NIACE

NIACE (1999) *A history of the development of NIACE*, NIACE briefing sheet No. 1, Leicester: NIACE

Open University. Committee on Continuing Education (1976) *Report of the Committee on Continuing Education*, Milton Keynes: Open University (Venables Report)

Parliament (1944) *Education Act 1944*, London: HMSO

Parliament (1992) *Further and Higher Education Act 1992*, London: HMSO

Piper, D. (1990) *Biography of Lord Clark*, Dictionary of National Biography, Vol. 1981–1985, 85–87, Oxford

Post Office (1962) *Broadcasting: memorandum on the Report of the Committee on Broadcasting, 1960*, London: HMSO

Reynolds, S. (2001) 'Credit, qualifications and the single framework for learning in Wales', *Adults Learning*, Vol. 12 No. 7, Leicester: NIACE

Robinson, J. (1982) *Learning over the air: 60 years of partnership in adult learning*, London: BBC

Sargant, N. (1991) *Learning and leisure: a study of adult participation in learning and its policy implications*, Leicester: NIACE

Sargant, N., Field, J., Francis, H., Schuller, T. and Tuckett, A. (1997) *The Learning Divide: a study of participation in adult learning in the United Kingdom*, Leicester: NIACE

Shawyer, R. C. (1944) *The Army Fights Illiteracy*, Adult Education, vol. XVII, No. 2, December 1944

Stamper A. (1998) *Rooms off the Corridor: education in the WI and 50 years of Denman College 1948–1998*, London: WI Books

Stock, A.K. (1977) 'Commentary', *Adult education*, Vol. 50 No. 4, Leicester: NIAE

Stock, A.K. (1980) *Adult education in the United Kingdom*, Leicester: NIAE

Stock, A.K. (1989) 'A Valediction for Adult Education', *Adult Education*, Vol. 61 No. 4, Leicester: NIACE

Taylor, J. (1978) 'The Advisory Council for Adult and Continuing Education', *Adult Education*, Vol. 51 No. 4, Leicester: NIAE

Thomas, B.B. (1971) *Biography of Dr. Thomas Jones* in Dictionary of National Biography, 1951–1960, 558–560, Oxford

Tuckett, A. (1988) *The jewel in the crown: adult education in Inner London*, London: ILEA

Tuckett, A. (2000) 'At the final hurdle', *Adults Learning*, Vol 11 No. 10, Leicester: NIACE

UDACE (1986) *The challenge of change: developing educational guidance for adults*, Leicester: NIACE

UDACE (1991) *Innovation in access*, Leicester: NIACE

Uden, T. (1996) *Widening participation: routes to a learning society*, Leicester: NIACE

Webb, B (1948) *Our Partnership*, 325–326 (passage date, 15 December 1905), Longman in Briggs, A (1962) *They Saw It Happen*, Oxford

Williams, W.E. (1971) 'Art for the people', *Adult Education*, Vol. 50 No. 4, Leicester: NIACE

Williams, W.E. (1960–1975) Personal letters to Lord Clark (sometime chair of the Arts Council) Arts Council Archive, Victoria and Albert Museum

Women In Peckham (1980) *I Want To Write It Down*, Peckham Publishing Project: London

Write First Time Collective (1978) *Let Loose*, Write First Time: London

Yeaxlee, B. (Ed) (1928–1929) *Handbook and Directory of Adult Education 1928-1929*, British Institute of Adult Education, John Ryland's Library, Manchester

Yeaxlee, B.A. (1929) *Lifelong education: a sketch of the range and significance of the adult education movement*, London: Cassell

ABBREVIATIONS

ABCA	Army Bureau of Current Affairs
ABE	Adult Basic Education
ACACE	Advisory Council for Adult Continuing Education
ACLF	Adult and Community Learning Fund
AE	Adult Education
AGM	Annual General Meeting
ALBSU	Adult Literacy and Basic Skills Unit
ALRA	Adult Literacy Resource Agency
ALU	Adult Literacy Unit
ALW	Adult Learners' Week
ARCA	Adult Residential Colleges Association
BA (Admin)	Bachelor of Arts (Administration)
BAS	British Association of Settlements
BBC	British Broadcasting Corporation
BCA	Bureau of Current Affairs
BIAE	British Institute of Adult Education
BSA	Basic Skills Agency
CAETA	Commonwealth Association for the Education and Training of Adults
CBE	Commander of the Order of the British Empire
CBI	Confederation of British Industry
CE	Community Education
CEMA	Committee for the Encouragement of Music and the Arts (later the Arts Council)
CPD	Continuing professional development
DACEE	Department of Adult Continuing Education and Extension (India)
DES	Department of Education and Science
DfEE	Department for Education and Employment

DfES	Department for Education and Skills
EBAE	European Bureau of Adult Education
ECA	Educational Centres Association
EDAP	Employee Development and Assistance Programme (Ford Motor Company)
ESG	Educational Support Grant
FAETBU	Forum for the Advancement of Education and Training for the Black Unemployed
FE	Further Education
FEDA	Further Education Development Agency
FEFC	Further Education Funding Council
FEFEA	Further Education Forum for the Education of Adults
FEU	Further Education Unit
HE	Higher Education
HMI	Her Majesty's Inspector
ICAE	International Council for Adult Education
IiP	Investors In People
ILEA	Inner London Education Authority
ILSCAE	International League for Social Commitment in Adult Education
ITA	Independent Television Authority
LA	Local Authority
LEA	Local Education Authority
LEAFEA	Local Education Authorities Forum for the Education of Adults
LRAM	Licentiate of the Royal Academy of Music
LSC	Learning and Skills Council
LSDA	Learning and Skills Development Agency
MBE	Member of the Order of the British Empire
MSC	Manpower Services Commission
NATFHE	National Association of Teachers in Further and Higher Education
NEGI	National Educational Guidance Initiative
NFAE	National Foundation for Adult Education
NFER	National Foundation for Educational Research
NFWI/WI	National Federation of Women's Institutes
NGO	Non-Governmental Organisation
NIACE	National Institute of Adult Continuing Education
NIACE Dysgu Cymru	National Institute of Adult Continuing Education – Learning Wales
NIAE	National Institute of Adult Education
NOCN	National Open College Network

OBE	Officer of the Order of the British Empire
OECD	Organisation for Economic Co-operation and Development
OU	Open University
PGCE	Post-Graduate Certificate in Education
REPLAN	REPLAN (not an acronym)
SOCRATES	SOCRATES (not an acronym)
TEC	Training and Enterprise Council
TGWU	Transport and General Workers Union
TUC	Trades Union Congress
UCAE	Universities' Council for Adult Education
UCNW	University College of North Wales
UDACE	Unit for the Development of Adult Continuing Education
Ufi	University for Industry
UNESCO	United Nations Education, Scientific and Cultural Organisation
WAAE	World Association for Adult Education
WEA	Workers' Educational Association
WJEC	Welsh Joint Education Committee
YE	Youth Education